P9-DHJ-686

FOLLOWING
THE
CARPENTER

FOLLOWING THE CARPENTER

DONALD E. WILDMON

THOMAS NELSON PUBLISHERS
Nashville • Atlanta • London • Vancouver

Copyright © 1997 by Donald E. Wildmon

All rights reserved. Written permission must be secured from the publisher to use or reproduce any part of this book, except for brief quotations in critical reviews or articles.

Published in Nashville, Tennessee, by Thomas Nelson, Inc., Publishers, and distributed in Canada by Word Communications, Ltd., Richmond, British Columbia, and in the United Kingdom by Word (UK), Ltd., Milton Keynes, England.

Unless otherwise noted, all Scripture quotations are from the New King James Version of the Bible, © 1979, 1980, 1982 by Thomas Nelson, Inc., Publishers.

Scripture quotations noted NASB are taken from THE NEW AMERICAN STANDARD BIBLE ®, © copyright The Lockman Foundation 1960, 1962, 1963, 1968, 1971, 1972, 1973, 1975, 1977. Used by permission.

Scripture quotations noted NIV are taken from the HOLY BIBLE, NEW INTERNATIONAL VERSION ®. Copyright © 1973, 1978, 1984 by International Bible Society. Used by permission of Zondervan Bible Publishing House. All rights reserved.

The "NIV" and "New International Version" trademarks are registered in the United States Patent and Trademark Office by International Bible Society. Use of either trademark requires the permission of International Bible Society.

Scripture quotations noted TEV are from TODAY'S ENGLISH VERSION copyright © American Bible Society 1966, 1971, 1976, 1992.

Scripture quotations noted J.B. PHILLIPS are from J.B. PHILLIPS: THE NEW TESTAMENT IN MODERN ENGLISH, Revised Edition. Copyright © J.B. Phillips 1958, 1960, 1972. Used by permission of Macmillan Publishing Co., Inc.

Living Thoughts, copyright by Donald E. Wildmon, 1971 & 1973, Five Star Publishers

Pebbles in the Sand, copyright by Donald E. Wildmon, 1970, Five Star Publishers

Springs of Faith, copyright by Donald E. Wildmon, 1971 & 1973, Five Star Publishers

Treasured Thoughts, copyright by Donald E. Wildmon, 1971, Five Star Publishers

Thoughts Worth Thinking, copyright by Donald E. Wildmon, 1968, Five Star Publishers

Stepping Stones, copyright by Donald E. Wildmon, 1971, Five Star Publishers

A Gift For the Graduate, copyright by Donald E. Wildmon, 1968, 1970, & 1973, Five Star Publishers

Nuggets of Gold, copyright by Donald E. Wildmon, 1970, Five Star Publishers

Practical Help For My Daily Living, copyright by Donald E. Wildmon, 1972, Five Star Publishers

All quoted material used by permission of the copyright holder.

Library of Congress Cataloging-in-Publication Data

Wildmon, Donald E.

Following the carpenter : parables to inspire obedience in the Christian life / Donald Wildmon.

p.   cm.

Collection of the author's writings previously published by Five Star publishers from 1968 to 1973.

Includes bibliographical references.

ISBN 0-7852-7215-1

1. Christian life—Methodist authors. I. Title.

BV4501.2.W5196 1997

248.4'876—dc21

96-49896

CIP

Printed in the United States of America

1 2 3 4 5 6 7 BVG 01 00 99 98 97

In appreciation to those faithful
supporters of *American Family Association*
who have stood with us through the years.

CONTENTS

PART I

FOLLOWING THE CARPENTER

SAYING OR DOING?

"Not everyone who says to Me, 'Lord, Lord,' shall enter the kingdom of heaven, but he who does the will of My Father in heaven."
(Matthew 7:21)

Let me tell you a true story.

Once there was a church that wanted to construct a new building. Inquiring around as to whom they could get to do a particular job in that construction, they were given the name of a certain man. The officials of the church called the man and asked him to do the job. Then the officials and the man settled on a fair price.

When the construction had gone far enough for the man to begin his work, the church officials had to call him three times to get him to the work site. He held up the progress for days. When he got to the site and on the job, he was met by the church's minister. The minister remembered meeting the man before at a downtown store, and he remembered that the man had impressed him as having an excellent knowledge of the Bible. Upon recognizing the man, the minister was sure that the church had gotten the best person for the job.

After the man had finished the first part of the job, he sent the church a bill. The total was considerably higher than the price that had been agreed upon, but the church officials said nothing and paid the full amount. "Perhaps this was to cover part of the labor to be done in the future," they thought.

When it was time to call the man to do the next phase of work, it took several phone calls to get him to the site. Again he held up the progress of other workers. Finally he came, but he did the job very slowly. The other workers had to do their work around him.

When it was time to call the man a third time and get him to complete his work so the finishing touches could be put on the building, he was even slower than before about responding. The church officials called him several times, and each time he promised he would be there the next day.

As they neared the date that the building was to be occupied, officials explained the situation to the man, and again he promised he would be finished and they could move in as scheduled. He came to the building, worked a short time, and left.

Finally, in desperation, the church officials hired another man to finish the job. They postponed their scheduled move into the building, as it was apparent that the inefficiency of the first man meant the building could not be occupied on time.

Now the second man who came to do the work didn't know much about the Bible, didn't teach a church school class, cursed incessantly, and smoked like a garbage pit. But he came promptly when called, worked quickly and efficiently, stayed overtime to speed progress, and presented the church with a reasonable bill when his work was completed.

A week after the scheduled date, the building was ready for occupation. The first man happened upon the job site, saw that someone else had completed the work, and went home and sent the church a second bill for far more than the agreed-upon price.

"Not everyone who says, 'Lord, Lord,' . . . but he who does . . .," said the Galilean. Now my question is, Which one of these fellows came nearer to living what the Carpenter taught?

WHEN TOMORROW COMES

"For we know that if our earthly house, this tent, is destroyed, we have a building from God, a house not made with hands, eternal in the heavens." (2 Corinthians 5:1)

Four-year-old Alison complained to her mom one day that her stomach hurt, so her parents took her to a doctor. The doctor came back from making an X ray and explained to Alison's parents why her stomach hurt. The X ray revealed that Alison had swallowed twenty-eight beads, a dog's bone, three plastic toy bricks, a deflated balloon, a toy dog, eight coins, some birdseed, a bit of sand, and several leaves. I would imagine that if I had all that in my stomach, I would have a stomachache too!

The story might startle us, or we might even find a touch of humor in it. But there is a higher truth that it brings to mind.

We are created in a certain way. The organs of our bodies are made to perform certain duties. Put food in our stomachs and we get energy to perform our work, fuel our brains, and build our bodies. But fill those same stomachs with junk—beads, bones, toys, balloons, coins, birdseed, sand, and leaves—and we'll end up with a tummyache.

Can we take this a step higher? Humans are made with another "part." We call it the spirit. Nurture that spirit and it will grow and give us the energy to perform good deeds for our Creator, our fellow human beings, and ourselves. But "feed" that spirit junk—pornography, violence—and we will end up with a spiritual "tummyache."

No adult with average intelligence would consume objects like those little Alison swallowed. Yet we willingly feed our souls a diet of spiritual junk. And we offer our children the same toxic diet.

Our lives can get so cluttered with things that have no lasting significance that we lose sight of those things that are most important. Eternity, for instance. Some people don't take it seriously. To them, the only important thing is the here and now. "Don't come around me with this Carpenter bit, preacher," they say. "I have a house, a good car, a good job, money in the bank, and booze in the cooler. I have everything I need."

Maybe they do have everything they need—for today. But how about tomorrow? What about eternity? When death comes, and it comes to everybody, will they have everything they need then?

Death—and eternity—may seem a long way off. But somehow it manages to get around to us. All of us.

JOHNNY SPENCE GOT WISE

"Men will be lovers of themselves . . . having a form of godliness but denying its power. And from such people turn away!"
(2 Timothy 3:2, 5)

There was a boy in South Carolina by the name of Johnny Spence. When he was thirteen he became a seventh-grade dropout. Like most dropouts, Johnny found life tough sailing. While he didn't have many talents, he did have one—golf—and he used it.

By the time Johnny was seventeen, he was the pro at a country club. Everybody liked Johnny. And for a seventeen-year-old, he made good money.

Johnny was a faithful church member, which meant that on Sundays he didn't show up for work until after church. One Sunday the president of the country club was waiting for him when he arrived at work. With him was the governor of South Carolina, the mayor, and others from the community's VIP list.

Asked where he'd been, Johnny replied that he'd gone to church. His superior remarked, "Well, you'll have to quit that or we'll find ourselves another pro. Being a church member is all right. I'm one myself. But don't let church interfere with business." So Johnny quit letting the church interfere with business.

Johnny soon became a golf instructor for some college coeds. He fell in love with one of the girls, and they began to go to parties. After a while Johnny's sweetheart began to criticize him for refusing to drink with the others. So to satisfy her, Johnny began drinking.

Things went real well for the seventh-grade dropout. It wasn't long before Johnny was making more money than he had ever imagined. He also became not only a heavy drinker but a drug user.

One day his wife and mother poured all his whiskey down the drain. Johnny grabbed the shotgun and would have killed them, he said later, if an officer hadn't hit him on the head from behind. Eventually, Johnny's wife and his mother admitted him to a hospital for help. When Johnny tried to end it all by slashing his wrist, a guard overpowered him.

While Johnny was in the hospital, a chaplain came to see him. The chaplain told Johnny that Jesus still loved him, wanted to help him, and would forgive all that he had done. Some Christian men from the country club where Johnny had worked came to visit him, pray with him, and express concern for him. Soon Johnny was going to their meetings. Before long he was once again a follower of the Carpenter, free of drugs and alcohol, and a person with a new lease on life.

Johnny Spence tells his story wherever people will listen to him. Many groups want him to speak about his recovery. But some who invite him to speak don't want him to mention Jesus' name in his story. They think it's inappropriate to mention Jesus outside of church. Funny thing is, it was this same type of people who helped get Johnny in a mess to start with. The only thing different now is that Johnny Spence is wise. He doesn't listen to them anymore.

Maybe one day we will all get wise.

MANY ROADS

"There are other sheep which belong to me that are not in this sheep pen. I must bring them, too; they will listen to my voice, and they will become one flock with one shepherd."
(John 10:16 TEV)

One of the joys of being a columnist and published author is the correspondence that comes from readers. I used to try to answer it all, but it soon became obvious that was an impossible task.

Some time ago I got a letter from a young soldier down at Fort Polk. He was from Monticello, Mississippi. I guess that letter meant about as much to me as any I've received. I laid it on my desk, fully intending to answer it and tell that soldier how much his few lines had lifted my spirits. But I lost the letter, so I wrote in my column that if he was still reading to please accept my thanks and apologies.

One of the amazing things about the bulk of the letters I receive is the number of denominations represented. They run the gamut of the various religious groups. And most of the writers feel as though I'm one of them. I appreciate that. For all of us who follow the

Carpenter of Galilee are brothers and sisters, regardless of our minor differences.

Quite often I get put out with some of my brethren in the ministry. All too often the emphasis in their messages is on division—what separates us from one another. What we need is not messages that will further divide us but those that will unite us and strengthen our kinship with each other. If God is our Father, then we are brothers and sisters. All of us.

The central theme of the New Testament is this: the Fatherhood of God and the brotherhood of humanity. If we could just grasp this truth and put it to work in our lives, we could do a lot to mend the wounds of the world. It's hard for most of us to hate members of our own family. Rather, we feel a responsibility for them and a desire to help them.

I like to think that I am a brother of everyone who calls God Father and follows Christ. To be sure, we aren't going to see eye-to-eye on theology. No two people see eye-to-eye on everything. But despite our differences, can't we strive to work together for the cause of the Carpenter?

As a young Mississippian, I often watched cotton farmers bringing their crops to the gin during the fall. Some would travel over gravel-covered roads from the East, their wagons full of cotton. Others would travel over narrow, paved roads from the North. Some came from the West, traveling on major highways. And still others came from the South, on a two-lane blacktop. When they got to the gin, the ginner never asked them which road they had taken to get to there. He simply asked, "How was your harvest?"

And that's what the Galilean Carpenter is going to ask.

WHAT DO YOU SAY WHEN YOU DIE?

"A man's pride will bring him low, / But the humble in spirit will retain honor."
(Proverbs 29:23)

His name was Thomas Jefferson. He was born at Shadwell, Virginia, on April 13, 1743. He died on July 4, 1826. The date seemed to be a tribute to the man. And in between those two dates he lived a life of service to his fellow human beings.

You probably remember him as the author of the Declaration of Independence. And most of all, he would have wanted you to remember him for that. His epitaph reflected that wish. Before his death, Jefferson instructed his daughter, Martha Randolph, to have these words inscribed on his headstone: "Here was buried Thomas Jefferson, author of the Declaration of American

Independence, of the Statute of Virginia for Religious Freedom, and father of the University of Virginia."

Those inscriptions say a lot about a man's life—any man's life. Jefferson's daughter could have put more on his headstone. She could have added a long list of accomplishments. He had served Virginia as governor. Most of us, had we had the honor of being governor, would have wanted others to know. He had been a member of Congress. But he chose not to mention that.

Jefferson could also have reminded those who viewed his headstone of the fact that he was minister to France and secretary of state in George Washington's administration. From there he moved up to vice president under John Adams. Had he wished, Jefferson could certainly have reminded future generations that he had been president of this country. But he didn't consider that accomplishment among his most significant.

Most of us would agree that pride is often a vice that destroys many. We accomplish something, and we cannot wait for the world to learn of our deed and praise us for it.

Why didn't Jefferson include all those other accomplishments on his headstone? He told his daughter the reason. "The things that are not on my inscription are the things the people did for me," he said. "The things that are on it are things I did for the people."

That's proper control of pride. Pray to God that we can all acquire it.

PRACTICING THE GOLDEN RULE

"And just as you want men to do to you, you also do to them likewise." (Luke 6:31)

Anthony Pino, age nine, came running into his house one afternoon, shouting to his mother that his three older brothers had fallen into the pond and needed help. It happened when one of Anthony's brothers, Ruben, jumped on a plank floating in the pond near their home and paddled away from the shore. He lost his grip and fell into the pond. When he called for help, two other brothers—Freddie, thirteen, and Richard, ten—jumped into the pond to save him.

As none of the boys could swim, Anthony ran to get his mother. Frantic, Mrs. Pino picked up the phone to call for help. Two people were talking on the party line. Mrs. Pino quickly explained the situation and asked them to please hang up so she could call for help. They refused. They laughed and ridiculed the frantic mother. She begged them again to get off the line, her boys were drowning. They refused to do so.

Another woman in the home with Mrs. Pino took the

receiver, spoke to the other two women, and besieged them to release the line. She, too, was refused.

Reading such a story, one wonders how any two people could be so heartless. A mother, pleading for the use of a phone for a few minutes to save her sons, was ridiculed and refused.

For thousands of years our Father has been trying to get us—all of us—to treat each other like brothers and sisters. And for an equal number of years we have been refusing. "Do unto others as you would have them do unto you." Stupid! Out-of-date! Childish! Some people evidently think so. I wish those people could speak with Freddie, Ruben, or Richard. Unfortunately, they can't. The boys drowned.

"Do unto others as you would have them do unto you." Think about it the next time you encounter someone in need.

WHEN YOU'RE WILLING TO LOSE

"For whoever desires to save his life will lose it, but whoever loses his life for My sake will save it." (Luke 9:24)

James O White, forty-four, thought his civilian job at McClellan Air Force Base was a waste of time and money. So, doing the opposite of what most folks would have done, White took pencil and paper in hand and wrote a suggestion for the suggestion box.

He told his superiors that the abolishment of his position as an inventory management specialist was in the best interest of all concerned. Now that's something the average person wouldn't do! We would try to hang on to our job as long as possible. But White wasn't the average person.

The suggestion slogged through bureaucratic channels for several months until it finally reached the Air Force Logistics Command at Wright-Patterson Air Force Base in Dayton, Ohio. And along the way it no doubt raised many an eyebrow and many a chuckle to boot. But at Wright-Patterson, someone appreciated White's idea and agreed with him. So, in a short time, his job was scrapped.

Luke 9:24 says that whoever loses himself will find himself. James White's actions were an example of that law being put into practice. He considered his job a burden on the taxpayers and saw a better way of getting the job done. And he was willing to risk his livelihood for the betterment of his employer. He got self out of the way and put a desire to do what was best above his own personal interests.

All of us should follow White's example. Many of us have never "lost ourselves." We think of ourselves as the number-one player in this game of life, and our thoughts hardly ever go beyond our own interests.

Years ago a Carpenter told some friends of His that if they would lose themselves they could find themselves. In fact, He said, one could never find one's true self until one had lost one's self. And He went on to say that the person who was continually looking out for number one would inevitably lose what he did have. The principle is true not only in a spiritual sense but in the whole of life. When we are ready to lose, then we are ready to find.

And what became of James O White? It's true that he lost his job, but he also received a check for a thousand dollars for his suggestion. And he was promoted to supervisor. He lost himself to find himself.

PART II

THE CARPENTER'S GUIDE TO LOVING RELATIONSHIPS

A WORD ABOUT WOMAN'S WORK

"First cleanse the inside of the cup and dish,
that the outside of them may be clean also."
(Matthew 23:26)

The other day I heard of a husband who requires his wife to keep the house spotless. Everything must be kept in place, clean, and in good working order. The meals have to be on the table at the right time, and the lawn has to be well-manicured.

Well, I used to be that way. When the house got messed up, I became upset. I used to use some unkind words to let Lynda know I wanted the house to look a little better. I say used to, because I've changed.

One day I walked into the house, and it was in a mess. I was all set to let go with the usual verbal barrage when I stopped to think things through. I thought about what Lynda had been doing all day. She had baked a cake for the neighbor up the street, which took up a good deal of her time. Then I thought of some of the other things she did regularly. She sewed the children's clothes in order to save us a little money. She cooked all our meals, washed dishes, did the laundry, and made sure the children were dressed properly for school. She drove the children to their dancing and swimming lessons, and she often baby-sat for another mother when she had to visit the doctor or run an errand.

Along with her household duties, Lynda was active in the church. She taught the children in church school and worked with the women's group. She tried to do her part for the different organizations we were involved in.

She had some of her own personal desires to fulfill as well, which every person has a right to do. And anytime anyone asked her to do something to help them or their cause, she consented.

Like I said, I changed. I realized that Lynda is a wonderful wife and a good mother. She is a friend to many and a servant of God. With four small children to care for and a sometimes-lazy husband to put up with, I decided that what she needed wasn't condemnation but recognition and commendation.

Our house gets pretty messy sometimes. The yard sometimes gets in a mess too. I used to wonder what other folks thought, but that doesn't bother me anymore. If they've been in the same situation they'll understand, and if they haven't, then all the explanations under God's sun wouldn't convince them.

Yes, our *house* gets messy sometimes. But that doesn't worry me because our *home* is pretty neat. And I will take a neat home and a messy house over a messy home and a neat house any day of the week.

A FOUR-LETTER WORD

"Love suffers long and is kind; love does not envy; love does not parade itself, is not puffed up; does not behave rudely, does not seek its own, is not provoked, thinks no evil; does not rejoice in iniquity . . . bears all things, believes all things, hopes all things, endures all things. Love never fails." (1 Corinthians 13:4–8)

Occasionally one comes across a story that speaks so loudly it cannot be ignored. This is such a story. Told beautifully and simply, it has endured through the years, though I no longer know who first told it. Here's the story:

"I have always had an abhorrence of funerals and dead people. When my dad died I flew back east for the service. As I viewed his cold, lifeless body in the casket, I felt nothing. That inanimate figure bore no resemblance to Pop, who had always been so happy-go-lucky and full of life.

"His strengths were also his weaknesses. His devil-may-care attitude made life a constant struggle for Mom. Pop was a traveling salesman but he was much better at traveling than he was at selling. In death, as in life, he left stacks of unpaid bills.

"When the moment came to close the casket, my heart

dropped as I saw Mom lean over and kiss him. Then she whispered in his ear, as she had done countless times before when he had left for trips: 'Bye, Pops. I'll be seeing you.' She was sending him off on his final journey—with the promise that she would join him.

"That gesture was an education for me. It told me more about Mother's love for Dad than anything I had witnessed in all my years at home. I wouldn't have missed it for the world."

There are a lot of folks in this world who carry signs and shout slogans about love. They get the headlines. There are others who quietly practice love, day in and day out.

Perhaps those who wish to have "trial marriages" could learn something from the wife mentioned in this story. It seems as though many people have decided to forget the "for worse" part of their marriage vows.

We have made a terrible mistake in judgment in our country. It is either the elite of society or the radicals who get the spotlight when love and marriage are the subject of discussion. Perhaps we should instead shine a light on people like the wife of this story. For it is that type of person who keeps our country together. Those who stick it out through thick and thin. Those who take their marriage vows seriously. Those who go on loving day in and day out without anybody shouting any cheers for them. Yes, it is the people whose love is genuine enough to carry them over the tough times that we are indebted to.

Love is a small word, just four letters. Yet it covers a multitude of sins and shortcomings.

FRIENDSHIP: A PRICELESS TREASURE

"A friend loves at all times." (Proverbs 17:17)

There is something of far more worth than fine gold. There is something to be treasured more than precious rubies. There is something that does more healing than all the miracle drugs. And, yes, there is something of more value than all the money this world offers.

What is this thing of which I speak? Why, friendship, of course. For the most precious thing a person can have is friends. And the more friends one has, the richer one is. Poor, indeed, is the person who is friendless.

How does one acquire friends? What magic formula can one use to get rich quick with friends? Well, the only way in the world that one can gain friends is to be friendly. You see, the old law that we've spurned is true. When we give, we get. When we give friendship, we get a friend.

But don't fool yourself into thinking that friendship is free. It most certainly is not. It is an expensive thing. It requires appreciation, time, and even the most costly of virtues—love. We must pay a high price for friendship. But in return, we get a high profit in friends.

Sometimes we miss the beauty of this thing we call friendship. How was it that Ralph Waldo Emerson said it? "The glory of friendship is not the outstretched hand, nor the kindly smile, nor the joy of companionship; it is the spiritual inspiration that comes to one when he discovers that someone else believes in him and is willing to trust him with his friendship." Friendship is spiritual inspiration that comes when someone believes in you, is pulling for you, and is willing to trust you to the utmost.

It lifts our sagging spirits to know that someone cares, that someone is concerned about us. I guess that's the reason we can never have a friend who is as good a friend as the Nazarene Carpenter. He cares about us. He trusts us. He believes in us. He is our greatest friend.

Friendship is born of love. Where there is no love, there can be no friendship. That's the reason His friendship is to be cherished above all others. For He didn't give up on us, even when we were at our worst—at the cross.

Someone has said that a friend is one who comes in when the whole world goes out. The rebellious young man we call the Prodigal Son learned who his friends were in this manner.

When everyone else has forsaken us, our friends will be beside us. That's what friends do. That's what Jesus did. He was called "a friend of publicans and sinners." When no one else would have anything to do with them, Jesus still loved them.

Friendship is priceless. So make all the friends you can. But remember this: To make a friend you must be a friend.

LITTLE JOHNNY

"Train up a child in the way he should go."
(Proverbs 22:6)

I saw a tragedy last Sunday morning. I hope I see it again next Sunday morning. Because I'd rather see the tragedy I saw than a greater one I fear will eventually occur.

The tragedy concerns a boy I'll call Johnny. Johnny is in elementary school, in his formative years. Johnny came to Sunday school and worship by himself last week. He's been doing it for some time now. Sometimes he rides with a neighbor. Sometimes he walks. Sometimes a member of his family brings him to the church and drops him off.

What's the tragedy? Just that. Someone in Johnny's family dropping him off to go in by himself. Johnny's father and mother have something "more important" to do. So Johnny goes to church, a place that would give him spiritual direction, all by himself.

The story is repeated often in our society. But I'm afraid it doesn't happen enough. For most Johnnys never manage to get to Sunday school and worship. They find more important things to do, like the rest of the family.

How long little Johnny will get himself to church, where he can get moral and spiritual instruction and guidance, I don't know. I hope he'll find the inner strength to continue the habit. But I'm afraid that one day Johnny will find it easier to sleep in. Or his family will make plans that will require Johnny to be away, and that will be followed by another Sunday with more plans, and another, and another.

What I'm saying is that the chance of his continuing his church-going habit is small. In all likelihood, he'll find that his visits to the house of God will have to cease, because the family has "more important things to do."

Johnny isn't a poor boy. His family is one of means. They have what most families want—two cars, a fine home, modern conveniences. His parents aren't millionaires, but they are well over the poverty line materially.

And that's the tragedy. Johnny's family gives him everything except what he needs most. And I guess, if you asked them, Johnny's parents would say they love him. Certainly there would be an emptiness in their home if Johnny were no longer there.

But like I said, Johnny's chances of continuing in church are slim. There's always a slight chance for a miracle, though. So I guess we can hope. But in a few years if Johnny doesn't make it and he turns out wrong, don't be too hard on him. Because, as a youngster, he really tried.

Johnny isn't kin to you, is he?

AS LITTLE CHILDREN

"Assuredly, I say to you, unless you are converted and become as little children, you will by no means enter the kingdom of heaven."
(Matthew 18:3)

The day had been a rough one. You know what I mean, for all of us have them. It seemed as though everything had gone wrong from the moment I'd gotten up. I had been on edge most of the day and so cranky that even I didn't like myself.

Then, to add to the woes of the day, it seemed as though my son had purposely been doing everything he shouldn't be doing. I was really grouchy with him. It just seemed like he was constantly in the way.

Why is it that we have days like that? I'm not completely certain, but I have some ideas. One is that we get in too big a hurry. Perhaps this is the biggest fault of our day and age. We go in such a rush we sometimes meet ourselves coming back! We think that our much-doing and fast-going means good living. We're wrong about that. Often what we need is to "be still and know."

Another reason we have days when everything goes wrong is because we don't take one thing at a time. We get a half-dozen things going—any one of which we should be doing by itself—and then they all demand our attention at once. We forget to take things one at a time. The result is tension and stress.

Still another reason for days when everything seems to go wrong is that we forget the eternal presence of the gentle Galilean Carpenter. We try to tackle all our problems, face all our situations, complete all our duties, alone. Life just wasn't meant to be that way. We are partners, not proprietors. And we need to remember that we are working with Him. We need to talk things over with our Silent Partner.

Well, my bad day finally came to a close, as they all do. After the children had their baths, it was time for our family prayers. I must admit I wasn't in the mood to say my prayers, and had it not been for the children I wouldn't have knelt down beside the bed that night.

For some reason that I can't recall now, the girls didn't say their prayers with us that night. It was just my son and me. I let him say his prayers first. I intended to say a quick one and call it quits.

He began in the usual manner, thanking God for several things. And then it happened. His tone of voice changed, and in his final petition, with a voice so sincere that I thought he was going to cry, he said, "And, dear God, make me a better little boy. Amen."

I was stunned and shocked, humbled and ashamed. It was my turn to pray now, and I had only one petition. It, too, came from the heart. "Dear God, make me a better father. Amen."

The Carpenter once said that those who enter His kingdom would have to come as a small child. I understand a little better now what He meant by that.

LIKE FATHER, LIKE SON

"Therefore you shall be perfect, just as your Father in heaven is perfect." (Matthew 5:48)

My study was located in a storage room directly behind our home. It was a small room to begin with, and once you put my books and supplies and machines in it you could hardly turn around. It was really too small, but it was the best we could come up with at the time, and I had to endure the cramped space until better days came along.

One day I was having one of those mornings when everything seemed to go wrong. It was a day when I and most folks around me wished that I had stayed in bed. My desk was covered with paperwork that needed to be done, my correspondence was lagging, and other matters were pressing for my attention.

I was sitting in my study, feeling overwhelmed with work and frustrated at my lack of space, when, without knocking, in came my son Timmy, who proceeded to sit down behind me. I started to turn and tell him there wasn't room for him in the study, but I waited, because I knew that if I spoke at that moment I would be harsh with him.

I continued working as he began taking paper from the wastebasket and books from the shelf. I jumped when he spoke.

"Daddy, do you have a pen?"

I reached into my pocket and silently handed him my pen. I then tried to continue my work. But it seemed that every time I turned around I bumped into him. So, with my temperature rising, I decided to scold him and send him back into the house. But turning to face him, I was stopped cold by what I saw.

Timmy had laid out before him some papers he had taken from the trash can and some books he had taken from the shelf, and with pen in hand he was marking on a sheet of paper. He had made himself a makeshift desk that was in something of a mess.

Now, most of the time when Timmy wants to know what I'm doing out in the study, I tell him, "I'm studying." While I looked at him there he paused for a moment and looked up, then after thinking a few seconds he began to write again.

"What are you doing, son?" I asked him.

He looked me in the eye as only a son can do and then gave me his answer with a little grin on his face. "I'm studying, Daddy."

I didn't say anything else to him. I turned back around and pretended to go back to work. But I didn't do much work for the next few minutes. I just sat there thinking how proud I was of my son. It made me feel just as big as a man can get to know that my son wanted to be like me, to do what I do.

But then a greater truth came to me. My Creator was telling me that this was really what He wanted from me. He wanted me to be like Him. I still think about that often. How good He must feel when we act like Him, do what He does, act like we are His children.

"Wouldn't it be a good world," I say to myself, "if we wanted to be like Him as much as Timmy wanted to be like his father."

It sure would.

THE ART OF LISTENING

"This is My commandment, that you love one another as I have loved you." (John 15:12)

I heard a story about a family that was eating dinner when the youngest member, a four year old, stood up in his chair and yelled, "Pass the butter!"

Of course his mother would have none of that. She turned to the child and said sharply, "We don't act like that around this house. You will ask for the butter politely or you will not have any butter at all. Anyone who acts like that doesn't deserve any dinner. Go to your room immediately!"

The little boy started to say something. "But . . ."

The mother broke in. "No but's about it. Go to your room at once!"

After supper, the father gathered the family together and told them he had a surprise for them. "I had the tape recorder on during the meal, and I want to play the tape so we can hear what we sound like while we are eating."

The family gathered round to listen to the recording. Supper began on a quiet note, but before long the group had gotten rather noisy. There was a lot of loud talking and laughing.

Then, as the mother listened closely, she thought she heard something. "Go back and play that part again," she told her husband.

He rewound the tape and played it again for her. Sure enough, there it was. A small, soft voice could barely be heard beneath the noise and laughter. It said, "Would someone please pass me the butter?"

The tape continued, and for a while all anyone could hear was the noise and laughter. Then, just a little louder than before, the voice spoke again. "Would someone please pass me the butter?" But there was no reply.

Then it happened. The voice boomed out, "Pass the butter!" And then came the mother's voice as she told him to go to his room without any supper. The mother stopped the tape, sent for the little boy, apologized to him, and gave him his supper.

I'm afraid there are many people like that little boy today. People who have tried to be heard in a nice way only to be ignored or have doors closed in their faces. If we had listened to the pleas for equality by African-Americans years ago, perhaps our race-relations problems wouldn't be as great today. And if we had listened to the workingman years ago, perhaps our unions would have better relations with management. But we were too busy with our own chatter.

One of the greatest skills we can learn is to listen. You see, listening shows we care. And, after all, that's what most people want. Someone to care.

Isn't that what families are for?

PART III

THE CARPENTER WILLS COURAGE

THE GREAT DREAM

"And it shall come to pass afterward / That I will pour out My Spirit on all flesh; / Your sons and your daughters shall prophesy, / Your old men shall dream dreams, / Your young men shall see visions." (Joel 2:28)

We used to be a nation of dreamers. Our forefathers, those who founded our country, were great dreamers. They dreamed of a country where people could be free, where they could live in dignity and hope and the promise of a better tomorrow.

They believed in that dream, believed in it so much they were willing to give their lives for it. Nothing could stop them from reaching out for that dream, not even the power of the king of England. They took that dream, and with it they beat the unbeatable foe. They conquered the unconquerable land. They traversed the impassable road. What great dreamers they were!

But they were not the greatest dreamers this world has had. There was a small group of men who had even bigger dreams than the founders of our country. Back nearly two thousand years ago there was a group of eleven men who had a dream, a great dream. They dreamed that they could conquer the world without ever lifting a sword or firing a gun. They dreamed that one day every man, woman, and child could and would share with them the new faith they had found. They dreamed that one day this world would be ruled by love.

It was a great dream they had. So great, in fact, that the world thought they were crazy. The world laughed at them, ridiculed them, even persecuted and killed them. But the dream could not be destroyed. It lived on. They planted that dream of a world ruled by love in the hearts and minds of others. And the dream took root and grew. Soon it had conquered the hearts of people of all nations, classes, and races.

There are those who are still dreaming that dream today. They are inspired by the same Carpenter who touched the hearts of the disciples. He has planted that dream in their hearts, nourished it, watched it grow. It is the dream of a world where men are brothers, where we help instead of hurt, share instead of steal, give instead of grab. It is a dream of a world ruled by love for one another.

A foolish dream? An unrealistic dream? An illogical dream? Yes, it has been called all of those things. But that doesn't stop people from dreaming it and from trying to make it come true. It is, in a way, an unfulfilled dream. But we still pursue it.

The call goes out from this Galilean Carpenter today for more dreamers. Few dare to give themselves to that dream. It seems unreachable to most people. It is certainly a big dream, and it requires the best there is in a person. For this reason, few dare to dream that dream. It is a challenge, the world's greatest challenge.

If you are a dreamer in search of a worthwhile dream, there is none greater in all the world. And one day, with His help, the dream will become true.

TRADITION

"He answered and said to them, 'Why do you also transgress the commandment of God because of your tradition?'" (Matthew 15:3)

Two men who lived in the villages of Djambi and Hasanuddin on tiny Haruku island in eastern Indonesia had a disagreement. Both of the men were stubborn, and each laid claim to a certain sago tree. Well, these two fellows decided to settle the question of ownership once and for all.

They decided to answer it in the traditional way—by seeing who could stay underwater the longest!

Now, to you and me this method may seem totally unrelated to the point in question. But for these two men, the fact that there was no relationship between the two didn't matter. Tradition decreed this was the way the question was to be answered. Questions had always been answered this way on Haruku. And as far as the men were concerned they would always be answered in this manner.

Tradition is, in many respects, a wonderful thing. It often preserves that which is good. We are greatly in debt to our parents and grandparents for some of the traditions they passed on to us. We think as we think and act as we act partly because of the traditions passed along to us.

But tradition is sometimes damaging and demeaning. Slavery lasted nearly nineteen hundred years beyond the life of the One who came to set men free because of tradition. A tradition no one questioned. A tradition that, thank God, is broken now. But the aftermath of that tradition lingers.

Tradition has said that when two countries come to an impasse, they must go to war, and the victor is "right." Might made right. After centuries of terrible wars, including the twentieth with its two world wars, this tradition is being increasingly questioned.

Each new generation is exactly that, a new generation. And each new generation should seek to carry on the good traditions of the past and end those traditions that we see to be harmful.

Now if this is a truth in the dealings of the world, then it is no less a truth in the work of the Church. There are many valid and worthwhile traditions in the Church. Likewise, there are traditions that need to be broken.

Someone has said that the seven last words of many churches are these: "We have always done it this way."

We don't like change. We prefer things to remain as they are. But there is one thing certain in this world—today is different from yesterday, and tomorrow will be different from today. And let us not forget how often the Founder of the Church broke tradition!

Let us, then, take the good traditions handed down to us and build on them. And let us have the courage to change those traditions that are no longer valid. If we fail to do this and hang on to tradition for tradition's sake, we will end up like those two villagers in Haruku. They both drowned.

THE DISCIPLES AT THE CROSS

"But all His acquaintances, and the women who followed Him from Galilee, stood at a distance, watching these things." (Luke 23:49)

We don't know how many of the disciples of Christ were present at the cross when

He was crucified. We infer from this passage of Scripture that perhaps several were.

We do know that the Crucifixion had a profound effect on the disciples. By piecing together the information we have about them at the time of the Crucifixion, we get a glimpse of what the Cross meant to them.

First of all, it meant bitter grief. The disciples were saddened over the death of their leader. They also felt a sense of futility. Had Jesus' death been by accident they could have accepted it. But to voluntarily give oneself over to one's enemies to be crucified as Jesus had done just didn't make sense. They dearly loved this Man, and His death seemed so senseless, so futile, so wasteful. It could have been avoided. He could have remained alive. But He chose to die.

In their three short years together the disciples had seen Jesus perform many miracles. They had seen Him raise people from the dead. They knew that He could have saved Himself. But He didn't. And that didn't make sense. He had actually let the Romans kill Him.

No more would they walk the Galilean hillsides, sail that little sea, or walk with Jesus down the streets of Jerusalem. No more would they share with Him the bread of life. All that was over now, finished. It was ended by the blows of a Roman soldier's hammer as it drove nails through Jesus' hands into a cross of wood.

The disciples were also remorseful, because of their cowardice in the face of injustice. They knew quite well that Jesus hadn't received justice, either from the Sanhedrin or from Pilate. They could have done something if they had only had the courage to do it. But at the time when Jesus needed them most, they lacked the courage to help Him. That, too, was perhaps running through their minds as they stood at a distance and watched this Man die on Calvary.

They longed for something they did not have—courage. They wanted so desperately to do something, anything, but they lacked the courage to even try. When it was over and His body hung lifelessly on the cross, they didn't even dare to ask permission to remove it for burial. A member of the Sanhedrin came to take the body down.

The disciples were cowards. They knew they were cowards, and they didn't have the courage to try to overcome their cowardice. They huddled together, afraid, behind locked doors.

The Cross also meant bitter disappointment for the disciples. They had left home, family, and jobs in the belief that this Carpenter was the Messiah. And it seemed now that He wasn't the Messiah. They had been following a false prophet. Jesus had done so much, performed so many miracles. They were so sure He was the Messiah. He had even said so Himself. But no Messiah would die on a cross between two criminals. So it seemed that they had been misled.

Jesus' death on the cross had convinced the disciples that He was not who they thought He was. For if He was the Messiah, He would not have let Himself be crucified. And if He was the Messiah, God would have intervened and stopped such a thing from happening.

But God didn't intervene. Therefore, Jesus was not the Son of God.

In their disappointment these disciples speculated that perhaps there was no just God at all. They had themselves witnessed a glaring example of injustice. And God had let it happen. No just God would let such a perfect man die at the hands of so great an injustice. Lies, hatred, and prejudice—a just God would have overruled these. But God hadn't. Therefore, simple logic said that there was no just God.

Now the disciples had to face the embarrassing humiliation, the ridicule, the scorn of the people who were their enemies. Before, when Jesus was with them, He had always managed to answer scornful comments with some eternal truth. When He was with them, they had been proud to be His followers. But now He was dead, and the facts had proven that the scribes and pharisees were correct. Now, wherever the disciples went for the rest of their lives, people would laugh and sneer at them. They would never be able to live this down. Their discipleship of this fallen leader was a social mark they would have to carry with them as long as they lived.

So you see, when the disciples descended the hillside on that Friday afternoon, their world had ended. A curtain had been drawn over their lives, and it was pitch black. There was no hope now, no promise that tomorrow would be any better, no belief that anything would ever be right again.

But then, on Sunday morning, something happened! God opened a whole new world! The tomb was empty!

It didn't take long for it to dawn on these men that while they had given up, God had continued to work. They had been defeated, but God had not. Instead of the world coming to an end, it was just beginning. Instead of shame and bitterness, hope and thankfulness and joy burst over the horizon with the morning sun. Slowly, ever so slowly, the truth was sinking in—God was using the foolishness of people in His plan of salvation. There was truth in the Cross that was now visible. And never again would that truth be hidden.

God, the disciples noted, had turned defeat into victory and tragedy into triumph. When these men were finally able to comprehend what had happened, something mysterious happened to them. No longer were they afraid. Or defeated. No longer did they go on meeting behind locked doors. They swung open the doors, walked into the streets of the whole world, and proclaimed a message of God's love.

Cowards? Not anymore. They were brave men, God's men. And neither the mighty force of the Roman armies nor all the lies that the scribes and pharisees told could ever again silence these men of courage. They were imprisoned, beaten, and stoned. But they never backed down, never bowed under. And the message they preached found life in the hearts of those who heard it.

Can you see what happened to these men? They were cowards before. One cannot deny that fact. The Bible doesn't try to hide it. But then they saw a risen Christ, and they became men of courage whom nothing, absolutely nothing, could stop.

To me, the most amazing thing about the Crucifixion wasn't the resurrection of Jesus, as truly astounding as that was. To me, it was the people to whom He entrusted His kingdom! Common people. This is the greatness of God, that His belief and trust in common people could not be daunted.

Do you think it could happen again, that the Spirit of Christ could touch us as it touched those disciples? Do you think it might be possible that God would once again entrust His work to people like you and me? Do you think that out of our deep love for this humble Galilean, God might be able to make an impact for good on this whole world?

Somehow I believe that He can.

BEING A PERSON OF VISION

"But Jesus said to them, 'A prophet is not without honor except in his own country, among his own relatives, and in his own house."
(Mark 6:4)

Mrs. Charles Hesse of Tripoli, Iowa, tells the following story:

"During World War I, my uncle was stationed as a ground mechanic at old Chanute Field in Illinois. One day his sergeant assigned him and two others to sweep out the hangar. While they were hard at work, a young lieutenant came in, sized up the situation, then asked them to push one small plane out, to move the others away from the doors, and to clear out.

"Climbing into the small plane, the lieutenant took off, circled the field, and a few minutes later, came back—thundering through the hangar and out again. Upon landing, his comment was, 'Sure beats sweeping.'

"The lieutenant's name? James Doolittle."

James (Jimmy) Doolittle is now part of the history of our nation. He was a man of vision. And being a man of vision brought him pain, persecution, and eventually a court-martial. Men of great vision who are willing to express themselves are often met with bitter opposition.

There was another man of vision who expressed Himself. He said that all people are important to the One who made us. He also said that when we live selfishly we shortchange ourselves. And He said that if we're not living like our Creator would have us live, we should change.

They executed this Man like a criminal. They hung Him on a wooden cross until the life was drained from Him.

We must not, any of us, dare to be persons of vision unless we're prepared to pay the sometimes high price. We mustn't dare to look carefully and searchingly into the future unless we believe in the goodness and kindness of the Creator and the steadfastness of His love.

James Doolittle, the army air hero, was a prophet. If that term sounds too religious for you then use the word *visionary*. Same thing. And being a prophet saps little people, people too weak to face their adversaries. That's how you can tell a true prophet from a false one. False prophets don't have the strength to meet the test; the true do. We don't have many prophets today. Or do we? Maybe we just don't recognize them as such. Maybe we're just calling them by other names—scientist, teacher, business executive, minister.

Doolittle's contemporaries laughed at him. They also court-martialed him. But later, they praised him.

Jesus' critics spat on Him. They also crucified Him. But later they worshiped Him. Both Doolittle and the Carpenter had something in their favor. They believed in themselves and in Something higher than themselves. That was their consolation.

Don't dare be a person of vision unless you're willing to let that be your consolation, also. Sometimes it's the only consolation you will have.

EXPENSIVE DECISIONS

"He steadfastly set His face to go to Jerusalem." (Luke 9:51)

Some things are terribly expensive. Lawrence of Arabia's book, entitled *The Mint*, was published after his death in 1935. Because he requested that it be withheld from the public until 1950, only ten copies were printed with the price tag of $500,000 per book! Can you imagine that? Five hundred thousand dollars for a single book. Most complete libraries aren't that expensive.

Yet there are things even more expensive than that book. Luke, the physician, records an example in the Scripture. Jesus' decision to "steadfastly set His face to go to Jerusalem" was far more expensive. It cost Him His life.

Jesus' entry into Jerusalem was a simple but dramatic scene. He was hailed as Lord and Master by those who loved Him. But in the background were those waiting for a chance to put Him to death. This tense situation was no accident. Great events are precipitated by great decisions.

Jesus was fully aware of the danger at hand. A difficult decision lay behind the Palm Sunday event. But He made it without wavering. A crisis was at hand in His ministry, and He met it magnificently. His decision marked Him as much more than a doer of good. It showed Him to be a man of great courage, strong convictions, and resolute determination.

We, today, could use a little more of those qualities. Most of us have them until it costs us something. Most of us are strong in our belief until a showdown is called for. Then we shy away, timid in the faith that once made us strong.

Why does it happen this way? We want to see right prevail. We want to see the gospel alive. But we don't want to get involved. We're apathetic. Faced with the situation that Jesus faced during His entry into Jerusalem, most of us would have said, "Let's go around the city and avoid the trouble."

Times of decision reveal our character as nothing else can. They separate the weak from the strong, the cowardly from the brave. Decisions are always before us. Shall we take the way of ease, escape, personal gain, and pleasure? Or will we choose the way of honor, sacrifice, love, and duty? Such decisions can't be sidestepped. The choices must be made.

If we don't decide, the decisions will be made for us. Time never stands still for our convenience. Either we "set our face toward Jerusalem" or we turn away. Only as we decide for God can we live on good terms with ourselves and our Master. We need to be thankful for the power of choice and for the chance we have to cast our lot with the people of God.

Some things in life *are* terribly expensive. Jesus' decision to face Jerusalem cost Him His life. But what other decision could He have made and still have been true to Himself and His God?

There are times when a decision to do right is going to cost you something. But we will never learn to live till we find something worth living for, and then stand solidly on that, whatever the cost. Have you found it yet?

WHAT COURAGE REALLY IS

"Joseph of Arimathea, a prominent council member, who was himself waiting for the kingdom of God, coming and taking courage, went in to Pilate and asked for the body of Jesus." (Mark 15:43)

You may have seen it. It was in the newspapers. The story of a young man who, in the process of saving the life of his baby sister, lost his life. His name was Walter Pittman. He and his family lived in Columbia, Mississippi.

The home of Leon Johnson caught on fire, and Johnson, his wife, their four children, and four grandchildren fled the fiery dwelling when the blaze was discovered. They were standing in the yard when young Walter discovered that his sister was not in the group and remained trapped in the house.

Walter darted unnoticed back into the house and managed to lead his three-year-old sister into a hallway of the eight-room house. There they became separated and, though she escaped, he burned to death.

Reading a story like that, I wonder about this virtue we call courage and the emotion we call fear. I believe Walter feared that fire as all of us would. What made him enter that burning building?

We make a mistake when we try to deny our fear. We think it's cowardly and even "sissy" to be afraid. So we pretend we aren't, and the psychiatrists end up with an office full of patients. Our mistake is that we're trying to rid ourselves of something we're supposed to have!

Fear is a God-given emotion. It is part of our humanness, just like all the other emotions we have. There's nothing wrong with it. Because it warns us of impending danger, it is, in itself, basically good. It is only when we misuse it, twist it, or ignore it that it's bad. We are supposed to be afraid sometimes. It is one of the surest safeguards we humans have against harm. Who isn't afraid if faced with a loaded gun? Who, upon sighting a tornado, doesn't seek cover? Only the foolish.

Courage isn't the absence of fear. Far from it. Courage

is the control of fear. So stop trying to rid yourself of fear. Just conquer it.

Take an example from Walter Pittman, who learned early. You see, Walter, the young man who gave his life saving his little sister, was only four years old.

PART IV

THE CARPENTER'S BRAND OF SUCCESS

NO HELP WANTED

"For I say, through the grace given to me, to everyone who is among you, not to think of himself more highly than he ought to think, but to think soberly." (Romans 12:3)

A young man named Bob walked into a service station. Seeing the station's owner in the rear, he yelled out, "Hi, Sam! How's business?"

From the back of the station came the reply, "As usual."

Sitting down next to the phone, Bob yelled again. "Mind if I use your phone?"

"No," came the reply. "Help yourself."

Bob picked up the phone directory and thumbed through its pages until he came to the correct listing. Placing the directory next to the phone, he dialed the number. About that time Sam walked up and sat down next to him.

"How are you doing with that new boat and motor, Bob?" he asked. "Folks been telling me that they're seeing a lot of Bob Smith out at the lake, hauling in the big 'uns. Sure sounds like you're getting your money's worth out of it."

Bob's party on the other end of the line had answered

by that time, and he held up his hand, motioning for Sam to be quiet. As Bob started talking, Sam noticed that he was disguising his voice to avoid being recognized. Wondering what it was all about, Sam listened closely to the conversation.

"Is this Woodruff's store?" Bob asked in the disguised voice. From the other end came the reply, "Yes, it is."

"Could I speak to Mr. Woodruff?" Bob asked in a muffled tone.

"This is Mr. Woodruff speaking," said the party on the other end.

"Mr. Woodruff, I was wondering about a possible job with you. Several months ago I saw an ad in the paper where you said you needed someone to work there in your store as a salesman. I have some experience as a salesman and believe I could do you a top-notch job," said Bob, as he continued to use the fake voice.

"I'm sorry," Mr. Woodruff replied, "but that job has been filled for about six months now. Fellow by the name of Bob Smith contacted us, and we hired him right away."

"Is that right?" Bob continued. "Sure hate to hear that. Would have loved to work for you. Maybe this Bob Smith fellow isn't doing too well and you could let him go and let me have that position?" Bob asked, while Sam stared at him with puzzlement.

"No, I'm afraid I couldn't do that," Mr. Woodruff replied. "Bob Smith is doing a real fine job. Fact of the business is that he's one of the best salesmen we've ever employed."

"Well, I appreciate talking to you Mr. Woodruff, and I may call you again in the future," Bob said as he hung up the phone.

Sam couldn't wait to ask the question. "What in the world were you doing, Bob? I thought you'd been working down at Woodruff's for about six months now."

"I have," replied Bob.

"Then why did you call about a job and talk in an unnatural voice?" asked Sam.

"Well, Sam," said Bob, "you might say I was just checking up on myself."

I guess that's something we all need to do now and then.

ON BEING RICH

"Life is more than food, and the body is more than clothing." (Luke 12:23)

A man once visited a certain home. The home wasn't much to look at, kind of run-down and lacking even a good coat of paint. In the yard, a little boy and his sister were playing. They were laughing and running, having a good time. The man surveyed the situation and surmised that the family wasn't very well off.

He asked the little boy some questions about his home and family. The little boy told him that his father hadn't been able to work lately because of illness, and that his mother had to take care of his dad. When asked about his patched clothes and bare feet, the youngster explained that he hadn't had any new clothes since his daddy got sick.

After a long conversation, the visitor found out that the little boy and his sister hadn't been to a movie or gone out for an ice-cream cone or experienced any of the normal childhood pleasures for several months. Wanting to say something to help the boy and his sister face the difficult situation, the man spoke. "It must be awful to be poor."

Quick as a flash the youngster answered, "Mister, we ain't poor. We just ain't got no money."

How true! How eternally true. He was happy. He loved his sister. His parents loved him. He knew why his family was in the shape it was in financially, and he didn't complain. Money couldn't have bought what he had.

How shallow our judgments are sometimes. How very misplaced our value of money. We think that only people who have money are rich.

We've made a terrible mistake in our thinking. And we have passed it on to our children. That mistake is thinking a person has to have a bankroll to be rich. What a terrible basis on which to judge richness. No one is poor who has character and purpose, whose life has been touched by the Galilean Carpenter, who has love of God and love of others.

The person who lacks those things is poor regardless of his or her bank account. Whoever uplifts civilization—though that person die penniless—is rich, and future generations will erect a living monument to him in deeds. A great bank account can never make anyone rich and can often hide real richness from view.

Someone is rich or poor according to what he is, not what he has. We are important because we are God's children, not because of our position or power or money. No one is rich who has a poor heart. One of the first great lessons of life is to learn the true estimate of values. How poor are those whose primary goal is a large bank account. A rich mind and a noble spirit cast over the humblest person a radiance that most millionaires will never know.

Don't pity the person who lacks money. Pity only the person who lacks character and purpose, who rejects the Galilean and the Father, who has no love for his fellow human beings. For that person is poor.

I'M A RICH MAN

"For you know the grace of our Lord Jesus Christ, that though He was rich, yet for your sakes He became poor, that you through His poverty might become rich."
(2 Corinthians 8:9)

I'm a rich man.

Some people, I know, will deny that. Looking at my salary, my bank account, and the possessions I have, most would by no means consider me rich. They wouldn't even go so far as to say that I was in the middle-income bracket, much less the upper bracket. But, like I said, I'm a rich man.

I'm rich because of my heritage. I came from a home where my parents loved me, provided for my needs to the best of their ability, sacrificed things they needed so I could have advantages they never had.

I'm a rich man. I have a wife who loves me. She puts up with all my faults, stands beside me, pulls for me when the going is rough. The stars in Hollywood couldn't hold a candle to her when it comes to real beauty.

I'm a rich man. I have a wonderful family. My children give me hope and the promise of a better tomorrow. I love them, want the best for them, and I find strength and love in them.

I'm a rich man. I have a job. A meaningful job. Not much money in it, or prestige. But it gives me a chance to help others, to lift their sights to a higher level, to give my life to a cause that will leave the world a better place in which to live. I will probably never reach the top of my profession, but I can face death knowing I did my best in the job I felt my Creator wanted me to do. I have a job I consider important, because He considers it important.

I'm a rich man. I live in a free country. Millions and millions of people long for the richness of that. They live in fear or under the shadow of a dictator. Millions more here in the country where I live have never realized that freedom is an obligation, not a license. Thus they are poor. Poor because they haven't learned that freedom is not a license to drag people into the depths of filth but an obligation to lift those around them to greater and greater heights, pressing on toward that higher goal to which our Maker calls us.

I'm a rich man. I have friends who are true friends. They stay with me through the good times and the bad. They encourage me to try harder. They keep me from giving up. When the clouds of darkness are around me, they are beside me, lighting the way. The doors to their homes are open to me, as mine are to them.

I'm a rich man. I've found what many are still searching for—forgiveness and understanding and help. I found them in a crucified Carpenter. He takes my weaknesses and makes me strong. He takes my fears and makes me brave. He takes my doubts and makes me believe. He assures me that I will have life after death.

Like I said, I'm a rich man.

REAPING WHAT WE SOW

"Do not be deceived, God is not mocked; for whatever a man sows, that he will also reap." (Galatians 6:7)

Human beings are prone to make mistakes. Some of the mistakes we make are very serious and costly. Some of them, however, are innocent and even humorous.

I heard once about a florist in Illinois. Somehow the cards on two bouquets were switched. A card attached to a birthday bouquet to a housewife from her husband read, "Congratulations. Hope the baby is doing fine." The other card, sent to a woman who had just given birth to her first child, read, "Twenty-seven! Hope you have many more!"

Well, it would be fine if all our mistakes were such humorous ones. Maybe we could laugh a little more. But the truth is that some of the mistakes we make are not so funny. Some of them are dead serious.

Paul, in a letter to the Christians in Galatia, wrote, "Make no mistake about this. God is not to be fooled; a man reaps what he sows."

Some time ago a parent expressed concern that her children didn't attend church as regularly as she wanted them to. And yet the parent attended church very seldom. We reap what we sow.

There is in the life that we live two roads on which we can travel—the high road or the low. There are natural consequences that follow the choice we make. The reason that the Carpenter came into this world was to get people to take the high road. And He came to lead us in our journey of life down that road. He will never force us to choose it, though. If we wish to choose the low road, He gives us the freedom to do so, even though it breaks His heart.

In the final analysis, we choose the kind of life we will live here on earth. People can influence us, but we have the final decision on what our life will be. Our lives are, after all, just about what we want them to be. And after we decide what we will do with our lives, we reap the results.

Yes, we make mistakes. Mistakes are the trademarks of humanity. But whatever else we may do, let us keep the truth of this in mind: "Make no mistake about this: God is not to be fooled; a man reaps what he sows. If he sows in the field of his lower nature, he will reap from it a harvest of corruption, but if he sows in the field of the Spirit, the Spirit will bring him a harvest of eternal life."

What kind of crop are you expecting?

WHAT OUR ORDERS ARE

"Do not love the world or the things in the world. If anyone loves the world, the love of the Father is not in him." (1 John 2:15)

Ethelwyn Wetherald wrote a poem once that expressed the thought, "I was not told to win or lose. My orders are to fight."

It's good to remember that today in the world in which we live. It seems that the measure of someone today is not whether he fights for what is right, but whether he "succeeds." Success. That's what we all want, and many are willing to pay dearly to obtain it. Success. That's what makes a person. Success. That's what gives meaning to life. Success. That's what rules the world.

Funny how we can take things and twist them to suit

our misperceptions, isn't it? The coach considered a success today is the one who wins the most games, not the one who teaches sportsmanship and love of the game. The doctor who is considered a success is the one who drives a big car and lives in a large house, not the one who relieves suffering. The business executive who is a success today is the one who has the biggest office or makes the most money, not the one who creates the largest number of jobs. Even a preacher of today isn't a success because he wins souls but because he pastors a large church.

Jesus, who was counted a failure by the standards of the world, said that the way to success was to serve. "The greatest among you shall be the one who serves the most," He said.

I think we need to get a few things in proper perspective. The Nazarene never once told us that we could expect success as the world measures it. He didn't even hint at it. He taught that we can expect the world to laugh at us and call us crazy, prudish, and stupid.

But we think we have to "succeed." And this has brought about a damaging and often damning attitude of compromise. We can't rid the world of liquor or stop some people from drinking it, so let's make it attractive. We can't rid the world of lust, so let's glamorize it and put it in an expensive magazine for everybody to see. We can't keep people from using the name of God in vain, so let's use it in the movies and on the radio and on television. Compromising is one of the deadliest sins of our day.

Abraham Lincoln once said it in these words: "I am not bound to win, but I am bound to be true. I am not bound to succeed, but I am bound to live up to what light I have. I must stand with anybody that stands right, stand with him while he is right, and part with him when he goes wrong."

Is it any wonder we say he was a great and successful man?

COMFORT OR CROSS?

"Then Jesus said to His disciples, 'If anyone desires to come after Me, let him deny himself, and take up his cross, and follow Me.'"
(Matthew 16:24)

The wording of the advertisement for church furniture revealed more about the Church than many people are aware of. It read: "Your Invitation To Worship In Comfort."

Isn't this the invitation the Church has been giving for the past couple of decades? "Come, worship in comfort." Our churches have been telling people this for years. We have tallied the reasons they should attend our church. And among the features we have advertised are those any good movie theater would list: Our building is air-conditioned, our service is entertaining, our seats are soft, and our requirements are few.

The result is that nearly half of those individuals who have their name on the church roll never enter the church door, and of those who do attend, only a small minority tote the financial load. Our rolls have never been so bulging or our buildings so empty. But at least we've "worshiped in comfort."

It seems as though I remember reading in the Bible something from the Carpenter about taking up a cross. It's been so long since I've heard it lifted up as a way of life that I sometimes think cross-bearing has gone out of style, if indeed, it was ever in. It's easier to become a member of some churches than it is to become a member of the local civic club, and it's harder to get out of church membership than it is to get out of most jails.

In some churches today, it's a good day if the crowd is large and the offering high. The preacher is successful if he serves a large church and makes a large salary. The "going" church is the one that claims the most people of means.

Sacrifice is out of style today. Security is in. It seems nearly an insult to ask someone to sacrifice his or her time, money, or talent.

"Your Invitation To Worship In Comfort." That's what's wrong with the Church today. We have done away with as many of the unpleasant requirements as possible. The result is that we have something that smacks of Christianity but denies its power.

Don't dare suggest that our church rolls should be an honest reflection of the number of people attending. You'd be seeking trouble, friend. I mean, after all, just because someone hasn't been there for twenty years, given a penny, or uttered a single prayer for the church is no reason he or she shouldn't be a member!

The Carpenter from Galilee didn't call us to statistical success. He didn't call us to build bigger buildings, to fill the roll book, or to water down the message. He called us to take up the cross, to be faithful, to issue the plea to those who would respond, and to go on loving those who didn't. The last time I read the words of Christ they were still, "Anyone who comes after Me must deny himself, take up the cross, and follow Me."

PART V

THE CARPENTER'S CALL TO SERVE

BEING SECOND-BEST

"Simon, whom He also named Peter, and Andrew his brother . . ." (Luke 6:14)

There's a game that most of us need to learn how to play. It's an exciting and rewarding game. And it's a game that nearly every person can play with good results. The name of the game is "How to Be Second-Best."

This game isn't a popular one. Most of us don't like to be second-best; we want to lead the parade. And there's nothing wrong with wanting to lead the parade. We wouldn't be worth much if we didn't want to be at the front of the march. But any schoolchild can tell you that a parade can only have a limited number of leaders. The rest must follow.

Not many of us know how to do that and do it well. Too many times we let our disappointment at being second-best turn into bitterness, and we become critical of the one who's leading.

All of us have had to play the role of second best at some point. Fact is, every one of us do it every day. No one can be a leader in everything. Everyone must follow in some things.

There were two brothers once who were commercial

fishermen. One brother was a natural leader. The other brother seemed destined to always be second-best. Whenever the two were introduced, the introduction went something like this: "Meet Peter and his brother, Andrew. They are fishermen." Andrew was always the last one mentioned. Even when Andrew wasn't with Peter, he was introduced like this: "Meet Andrew, the brother of Peter." No matter where Andrew went, he was always second-best, always Peter's brother.

But being second-best didn't destroy Andrew or make him bitter. Anyone who knows the story of these brothers knows that Peter was what he was because of Andrew.

There are some truths that we need to learn in order to succeed at being second-best. First of all, we must remember that second-best doesn't necessarily signify second-rate, or someone of less importance. The backfielder does all the scoring and gets all the publicity, but he will be the first to tell you of the contribution of the players up front.

Then, too, being second-best doesn't mean we can't do our best. And if someone does his or her best, no one can ask for more, regardless of what others are able to do. Real judgment comes not from comparing ourselves to another, but from comparing our results to our potential. For it is evident that not all of us have the same talents.

Andrew was wonderful at being second-best in the game of life. The thing that made him great was his deep-rooted humility. And unless we have that virtue, we will never be able to play the game at all.

UNCOMMON COMMON PEOPLE

"And the common people heard Him gladly." (Mark 12:37)

Something unusual happened in Zurich, Switzerland. Billboards announced that a man named Anton Sergeivitch Tartarov was to give a piano concert. They said that Tartarov was an internationally known Russian pianist.

This concert ended a little differently from most, however. After his performance, Tartarov received a standing ovation, cheers, and shouts for encores from the thousands present. When the crowd stopped cheering and the impresario stepped up to speak, he told those present that the pianist wasn't really Tartarov. There was no such person. Furthermore, he said, the pianist wasn't Russian, but Swiss. To further complicate matters, he announced that the numbers the pianist had played were not the announced compositions by Beethoven, Prokofiev, and Liszt but the arrangements of the pianist, Jean-Jacques Hauser!

The crowd still wanted the encore. Hauser gave it to them gladly. The man responsible for the show told the audience that he had invented Tartarov "to give Hauser an audience free of prejudices."

You see, most of us, though we're perceived as "common people," have some uncommon talent, something that we can do well—sometimes better than anyone else in the world. But because of prejudice—our own or that of people around us—our talent often remains hidden.

And that brings us around to the Galilean. He brought out the greatness in common people. Someone has said that characteristic is what got Him placed on the cross. He lacks the prejudices that we so often have. He lifts the common person, makes us important, even great—as a servant.

Remember, Jesus Himself was a "common man," a carpenter. He made things with His hands. But one day this Carpenter ceased working on wood and began working on the hearts of people. He went to the common person and shared a message that was "heard gladly," that put hope and love in the hearts of hearers. And we haven't been the same since.

As the people in Hauser's audience learned, when viewed without prejudices, even an unknown, a "common man," can achieve greatness.

KEEP MEANING IN LIFE

"The Father loves me because I am willing to give up my life, in order that I may receive it back again." (John 10:17 TEV)

In the spring of 1972, actor George Sanders took a vacation in a resort area of Spain. At the time Sanders was sixty-five years old. He had what many people work for in life. He had fame and fortune. He had a good education. And he had good health for a person his age.

Yet, while on that vacation George Sanders committed suicide. On the note he left behind he stated: "I am bored and have already lived enough."

There are many people who feel that way. Life has lost its meaning and, as a result, they've lost the desire to go on living. It happens to many of us, especially when our purpose for living doesn't stretch beyond ourselves.

There is a great truth running through the fiber of life. That truth is that our zest for living disappears when a purpose for living doesn't exist. For life to have meaning, a person must find purpose in it. Without purpose, nothing really matters. And that purpose, if it is to keep us going, must be above and beyond ourselves.

The Carpenter from Nazareth laid it out in a simple

way when He said, "The person who loses his life for My sake shall find it." When you have committed yourself to building a better world, to working for our Creator, to helping the human race learn to love and help each other, then life is always worth living.

Despite the opinion to the contrary, fame and fortune do not, of themselves, infuse purpose and meaning into life. Few poor people commit suicide. They have to keep going because someone is depending on them.

Lose your life in service to your fellow human beings, give yourself over to making the world a better place, follow the advice of that Galilean Carpenter, and you will find life. Life with meaning and purpose, life full of zest.

The person who lives only for himself will one day become bored and grow tired of it all. Eventually the meaning of existence will disappear. Then there will be no desire to press on.

"The person who loses his life for My sake shall find it." There is a world of truth in that statement. The person who heeds its truth will never lose the purpose for or meaning of life. The person who ignores it will often die years before he is buried.

Lee Rosten, writing in the *Library Journal* said, "The purpose of life is not to be happy, but to matter, to be productive, to be useful, to have it make some difference that you lived at all."

A person striving to make the world a better place in which to live doesn't have time to become bored.

GIVE AND IT WILL BE GIVEN

"Give, and it will be given to you: good measure, pressed down, shaken together, and running over will be put into your bosom."
(Luke 6:38)

Several years ago there was a young drifter in Australia by the name of Tom Ellis. One day Ellis picked up a discarded newspaper and saw an ad about a correspondence course in electricity. Although he had no money and the correspondence school was in America, Ellis wrote to the school seeking enrollment. He appealed directly to Fenton Howard, the man in charge of the school. Howard allowed Ellis to enroll in the electronics course, despite the fact that there was a chance the school would never get a penny in tuition from Ellis.

It was an act of kindness on the part of Howard. He was trying to help someone who was trying to help himself. It was through that course, and the kindness of Fenton Howard, that Tom Ellis learned a life's trade. He stayed with the course for several years before World War II broke out. Then he enlisted in the Australian navy.

A kind act, done for someone else, has far-reaching

effects. Life is designed so that when you help another person you help all people, including yourself. What was it that the Carpenter taught in Matthew 10:42 about giving a stranger a cup of cold water? "Whosoever gives . . . a cup of cold water in the name of a disciple . . . shall by no means lose his reward." You see it is a very practical way of living.

During World War II, Fenton Howard was wounded while serving in the Pacific. The ship on which he served as a naval electrician had been disabled. A shell had damaged the generator and crippled the ship's power supply. An electrician was desperately needed to do some repair work on the ship, or Howard's chance of survival would be slim.

An SOS distress signal was sent out, and an Australian ship nearby came to the rescue of the disabled ship. The electrician from the Australian ship came on board and repaired the damaged generator, making it possible for the American ship to sail for home. The act of repairing the generator saved the life of Fenton Howard.

You've probably already figured out that the Australian electrician was Tom Ellis, the same Tom Ellis whom Fenton Howard had helped years before.

Writing in Ecclesiastes, an old preacher by the name of Koheleth said it this way. "Cast your bread upon the waters, for you will find it after many days." Centuries later the Author of Life put it this way: "Give, and it will be given to you."

A kind act, done for another, has far-reaching effects.

LIVING PICTURE

"So the King will greatly desire your beauty."
(Psalm 45:11)

Around the year 1490 there were two young artists who were very good friends. Both of them were poor, and that meant they had to support themselves while they studied art. Because their jobs took so much of their time and energy, their advancement in the field of art was slow. Discussing their plight, they struck an agreement. They would draw straws, they decided, and the one who drew the longer straw would study while the other worked to support both of them.

The young artist who drew the longer straw went to the cities of Europe to study. History records that he soon became recognized as one of the outstanding artists of his time.

After gaining success, he went home to get his friend and let him come to Europe to study while he, the successful artist, supported both men on his earnings.

When the man who had become a recognized artist saw his friend again, he discovered that the hard manual labor his friend had to perform had caused his fingers to become stiff and bent. He was no longer able to execute the delicate brush strokes necessary for painting. It was apparent that his dream of becoming a successful artist could never come true.

But the successful artist noticed an unusual trait in his friend. The friend accepted his fate without bitterness, happy that he had played a part in the success of the other man. He actually rejoiced in his friend's success.

One day the artist came upon his friend unexpectedly as he knelt in prayer. He was praying for the success of his friend, although he himself could no longer realize his own dream. Something about the kneeling man caught the attention of the artist and he hurriedly sketched the hands folded in prayer. Later, the artist took that sketch and from it drew one of the most famous paintings in the world.

The man who painted the hands was Albrecht Dürer. The man whose hands he painted was Franz Knigstein. And the painting is known today as *The Praying Hands*.

The beauty and inspiration of *The Praying Hands* come from the life that made it possible. You see, creating a painting of sacrifice and serenity isn't nearly as important as living one.

PART VI

THE CARPENTER AND CULTURE

THE GUILTY GO FREE

"Brood of vipers! How can you, being evil, speak good things? For out of the abundance of the heart the mouth speaks." (Matthew 12:34)

It wasn't headline news, but it might have served a good purpose if it had been. It was the story of Juergen Peters. Sensation-hungry spectators, disappointed when the nineteen-year-old gas station attendant abandoned his suicide attempt, taunted him into jumping to his death from a one-hundred-foot water tower.

A fire department official said that the youth climbed an iron ladder to the top of the tower and threatened to commit suicide following a dispute at the gas station where he worked. He changed his mind and was climbing back down when the taunts began.

"Jump, you coward, jump!" someone shouted from the crowd. As Peters moved lower, the taunts became louder. He hesitated, looked at the crowd, then began to make his way back to the top. There he climbed onto a parapet and threw himself off.

I'm sure the crowd went home with a sense of satisfaction, real fulfillment. They must have felt the same sick thrill the Romans used to feel when Christians were thrown to the lions. The sight of twisted, broken, bloody humanity must be an enjoyable sight to such people.

We boast a lot about living in a civilized society. We brag on our scientific advances and revel in our electronic accomplishments. We have learned more in the past ten years than the human race learned in all of recorded history up to that time. And yet, with all of our marvelous wonders, we're sometimes nothing more than bloodthirsty monsters.

We have counted the Church out in our world. There's no place for Him, not in our modern society. He was a good crutch for the ignorant ages gone by, but the myth of Him just doesn't hold up today. Few, indeed, are those who really believe that He has anything to offer our age. Most people have "outgrown" the need for Him.

Let us suppose—and I know it is purely speculation—but let us suppose that those people who stood on the sidewalk beneath young Juergen Peters were followers of The Way, had decided to live by His will. Peters would be alive today. Have we outgrown Him? Or have we merely become more ignorant with all of our learning?

Well, one thing is clear when you look at the incident. All murderers aren't arrested. Some can walk away, perhaps to taunt—and kill—again.

GETTING USED TO THE DARK

"Lest Satan should take advantage of us; for we are not ignorant of his devices."
(2 Corinthians 2:11)

I went to the movies recently. It was the first time in a long time that I'd been. I'm not about to spend my hard-earned money to see filth portrayed as the ideal. But there was a children's movie playing, so I took my kids and enjoyed it.

As I entered the theater, it was dark and I could hardly see. I moved slowly down the aisle and found a row where a seat was empty—or so I thought! After sitting in someone else's lap for a split second, I hurriedly fumbled on down the row to an empty seat. Talk about dark!

But something happened to the darkness in that theater. After I had been in the blackness a short period, I began to get accustomed to it. Why, I could even make out which seats were empty. It wasn't long before that theater didn't seem too dark at all. I could find my way around without a bit of trouble.

Something like this has happened in our society, our culture. The darkness seems so dark at first, but if you sit in it long enough, you get the impression that it isn't so dark after all. Time was when sin was called sin, when you could tell the good from the bad, but that time is slowly disappearing. We have sat in the darkness until we've gotten used to it, even gotten the false impression that new light is breaking.

Alcoholism carries no moral overtones today. It has a new name—addiction. An alcoholic now is a sick person, not a sinful one. We used to call alcoholism sin, but now it's a disease, a disease that we manufacture, bottle, advertise, sell, regulate, and collect taxes on. Are we getting used to the darkness?

In the sixties, adultery got a new name—free love. And it has many advocates, both in and out of the Church. It isn't sin anymore; it's the result of situational ethics. A movie star or rock idol can have a baby out of wedlock one week and gain the admiration of millions the next. Are we getting used to the darkness?

Murder will get you a hung jury and sometimes three years in prison at the most. And if you can afford the right lawyer, you can go scot-free. We are a little more "civilized" than our forefathers. We believe in being lenient. The darkness is getting brighter now.

Strange, isn't it, that we don't get used to the darkness all at once. We have to sit in it a while. Then it doesn't look dark anymore. Slowly, little by little, we get used to it.

But the Light of the World is still in the world, and people who love good and hate evil are still attracted to Him. And, strange as it may seem, people who love evil still hate the Light. For you see, when the Light comes they have no place to hide.

CHANGING TIMES

"There were also false prophets among the people, even as there will be false teachers among you." (2 Peter 2:1)

Air Force Master Sergeant Lee J. Kenney had a habit common among enlisted personnel. He liked to collect military souvenirs for his kids. One day Kenney happened upon two bazooka-type shells on the bomb range at the old Salina, Kansas, air base. He took the shells to a weapons expert to be sure they were safe. After the expert gave him the go-ahead, he carried the mementos home.

Kenney's two boys, ages 11 and 13, took a liking to the shells. They kept them around the house for about a year. Then one day they and some of the other neighborhood children decided they would like to play soldier.

Have you ever noticed that some things that were once considered harmful are not believed to be so now?

Today they are only amusements, things many people like to play around with.

Consider alcohol. It used to be considered harmful. Now society treats it as though it were harmless, and a great many folks have a lot of fun playing around with it.

Then there is this thing of illegal drugs. Many of us can remember when drugs were considered dangerous. But a great number of folks, young and old alike, have decided that drugs aren't nearly as dangerous as we once thought they were. And they're playing around with them.

Another thing that comes to mind while thinking along this line is our modern attitude toward sex. Some of us can remember when sex was considered a wholesome and binding experience that was to be confined to the bounds of marriage. We knew, also, that outside of marriage, sex could have dangerous consequences. But modern-day advocates of free love evidently believe us "old fogies" are wrong. Because everywhere you turn today sex is portrayed as something to make a game of.

When I read the story of MSgt. Kenney's "toy" shells I thought about all that. Jonathan and Timothy Kellogg, ages 11 and 9, and Donald Brown, 9, and David Hasen, 8, were having the time of their life with the shells. That is, until one of the shells exploded and killed all four boys.

Experts have changed our ideas about several things. Are experts ever wrong?

GREAT INFLUENCE

"For false christs and false prophets will rise."
(Matthew 24:24)

I'd like to share with you some information on two men who have had great influence on the world in which we live.

The first man was born of Jewish parents. Later his parents embraced Christianity. He was brought up with a good formal education and earned a doctorate from a university. Despite a formal education, he spent most of his life in poverty.

During his entire life he had only one close friend, a fellow who shared some of his views. He was a prolific writer and a man of strong beliefs. He was twice driven from his country because of his expressed views. He changed society little while he was alive, but after his death his followers shaped nearly half the world.

The other man was also born of Jewish parents. His mother later embraced Christianity, also. He had little formal education and had to learn a trade that his father taught him. He, too, spent a good share of his life living in poverty.

He had few close friends and the few he had deserted him when he needed their friendship most. They tried to share his views but found it hard when some continually called him a fool. Although he was never driven forcefully from his own country, he was asked to leave another country because its citizens were afraid of what he was doing. Like the first man, this man changed little of society while he was alive. But since his death, his followers have shaped their share of the world.

The first man died a natural death in his old age. The second man died because of the tremendous hatred some people had for him. The method of his death was capital punishment. The first man advocated force to change society to fit the mold he thought it should be. The second man never attempted to change society but rather sought to change individuals. The first man was concerned mainly with the masses. The second man was concerned mainly with the individual.

While the first man left us volumes of his writings to study, the second man never wrote a book. If it hadn't been for his friends and their concern for his teaching there is a possibility we would never have heard of him. Both of these men wanted to see world change.

Centuries later, the systems that grew from the life and teachings of those two men stood face-to-face around the world. The men? The first was Karl Marx, the father of communism. The second was Jesus of Nazareth, the Father of Christianity.

SEEKING HAPPINESS IN THE LITTLE PILL

"But seek first the kingdom of God and His righteousness, and all these things shall be added to you." (Matthew 6:33)

It's a funny age in which we live. We have more now than any people in the history of the human race. We earn the highest wages, eat the best food, wear the finest clothes, live in well-constructed houses, travel farther by faster and more comfortable means, retire earlier, and live longer. All this, yet we are, in some respects, the most miserable people ever!

The American Chemical Society estimates that Americans use $32 million worth of tranquilizers every year. Another $25 million worth is given to patients in mental hospitals. And, listen to this: One out of twelve Americans takes tranquilizers regularly.

Dr. Herbert Ratner says that America is the most overmedicated and yet most anxiety-ridden country in the world. We suffer from so-called diseases of civilization, including neuroses, high blood pressure, ulcers, and heart disease. And here is a fact that's appalling to any sensible person: Suicide is the fourth-leading cause of all deaths in people between the ages of fifteen and forty-four and is growing in prevalence among teens. In the years in which life is supposed to be the most care-free, suicide ranks fourth as the cause of death! The trouble, according to Dr. Ratner, is that we look at mental and physical health as a commodity to be bought in a drugstore. "We have become increasingly a paying animal," he says, "whereas we have become decreasingly a praying animal, as if spiritual repose were unrelated to total health."

Sound physical and mental health don't complete the person. They will any other animal, but not the human being. We have a spiritual side that is far more important than the physical or mental. Whether we are willing to admit it or not, mind and body and spirit affect one another, for good or ill.

The Carpenter of Galilee had something to say about this. "Seek first His kingdom and His righteousness," He said, "and all these things shall be added to you." He knew that happiness comes from wholeness. This is one interpretation of the Beatitudes. "Blessed are they," He said. He's saying that the happiest people are those who relate themselves to others, to their world, to their Creator, and to themselves in the way He intended.

It's ironic indeed that those who are desperately seeking happiness never find it, and those who are too busy doing something worthwhile to seek happiness are the most happy.

It's true, then, that the words of the Carpenter of Nazareth shared nearly two thousand years ago still ring true today, and many who have failed to find comfort in tranquilizers have come to find truth in them.

"Seek first His kingdom and His righteousness, and all these things shall be yours as well." Give these words a try in your life. You'll be mighty glad you did.

PART VII

THE CARPENTER'S QUIET HEROES

THE WORLD MAY NOT KNOW YOUR NAME

"For I know their works and their thoughts."
(Isaiah 66:18)

I recall a poem from my high school days about a man by the name of Paul Revere. It began something like this: "Listen my children and you shall hear / Of the midnight ride of Paul Revere."

There was another person who made a similar ride during that War of Independence. I doubt that you've ever heard of her. Her name was Sybil Ludington. She was only sixteen years of age the night her father received a message that the British had just destroyed a neighboring city and were advancing toward their home.

Sybil volunteered to ride through the countryside in the middle of the night to warn residents of the approaching enemy and to call them to arms in defense. All night Sybil rode, going from farmhouse to farmhouse, warning the farmers that the British soldiers were advancing and telling them to prepare for battle.

When we compare the two rides, we discover that the poet perhaps did an injustice by writing of Paul Revere. For Paul Revere rode only ten miles in his famous ride.

Sybil Ludington rode about forty. And her ride was far more effective.

The comparison points out something we need to remember in life. It isn't always the person who gets the greatest acclaim who's done the most good. Many people who have made outstanding and lasting contributions to society are known to only a few.

Don't think that the contribution you make isn't important simply because your name isn't spread across the country in the mass media. For despite what we think, those who make the headlines are not the only ones who contribute to the good of the world. More often than not, they aren't even the major ones.

If fate should happen to give you the reward of public recognition for the good you do, well and good. But if not, just remember that your contribution is in no way diminished simply because the world doesn't know your name.

After all, the reason we do the good we do isn't to gain public recognition. We do it because we know it's what we should do. In fact, a person who gets angry because he fails to gain recognition for something he has contributed to society really isn't a person who needs publicity.

Above us, keeping watch over us, is One who sees the good we do. He isn't impressed by the headlines. But He is impressed when we do the best we can with what we have. And it's His recognition, not the public's, that really matters after all is said and done.

Although the world may not know your name, just remember that He does.

IT WAS JUST GUS

"He has shown you, O man, what is good; / And what does the LORD require of you / But to do justly, / To love mercy, / And to walk humbly with your God?" (Micah 6:8)

Near Dublin, England, a young preacher started a revival meeting in a barn. Folks who attended said it was a rather discouraging meeting. It didn't last long. The preacher simply stopped the service, packed up his bag, and moved on to what he considered more fruitful fields.

Only a few folks turned out for those meetings, and they weren't much interested in the services. There was one young boy—Augustus M. Toplady—who made a decision for the Galilean Carpenter during the meetings, but no one paid him much attention. It was just Gus. And the crowd hardly got excited when Gus made his decision.

Strange, indeed, are the ways we measure success. Numbers. Statistics. That's the only method many of us use to judge the worth of a venture. So we count as failures those ventures where we're not overwhelmed with "numerically quantifiable" success. If the leading citizens of the community had come to that meeting back in Dublin, if they'd decided to become followers of the Way, the meetings would have been judged a success. They would have been continued. But just Gus? Why, it seemed a waste of time.

A fellow told me that hindsight is a whole lot better than foresight. The only problem is that by the time we get to a place of hindsight, we have already followed our foresight!

I remember a story about another Man who made a decision. His community didn't get too excited about it, either. This Man decided to become a preacher. When He returned to his hometown to preach, many of the people wouldn't listen to Him. Do you know why? It wasn't because He didn't have anything to say. He did. It was because of who He was. "Is this not the carpenter's son?" they asked. And because He was the carpenter's son and not the son of the high priest, the people wouldn't listen to what he had to say. Instead, they ran Him out of town following a sermon in which He preached a view unpopular with them.

Well, young Gus also grew up and turned out to be a preacher. He wrote several books, despite the fact that he died when he was only thirty-eight. Those books are out of print now and long since forgotten. He also preached many times. More than a thousand sermons in all. But his sermons aren't remembered now. And Gus liked to write songs. He wrote 133 in all. Most of them haven't survived the years since Gus was around.

But one song that Gus wrote has survived the years. And it gives every indication of surviving many, many more. This song can be found in nearly every hymnbook you pick up. It's entitled "Rock of Ages." It's a favorite of millions and has been a source of inspiration to countless numbers.

Augustus M. Toplady shot a hole in the theory that success can only be measured in numbers.

A LITTLE BOY, BUT A BIG MAN

"Blessed are those who are persecuted for righteousness' sake, / For theirs is the kingdom of heaven." (Matthew 5:10)

Emmanuel Dannan had a difficult life. He lost his parents when he was four years old, and he was placed in the Milwaukee poorhouse. He spent his next three years in that institution. Then Mr. and Mrs. Samuel Norton adopted him. The Nortons adopted a girl, two years older, at the same time they adopted Emmanuel. The children went to live with the Nortons on the farm in Marquette County.

Emmanuel had been living with the Nortons for about a year when Mr. Norton, whom he called "Pa," told the lad of eight to tell a lie about something. The boy responded, "Pa, I don't lie."

When Emmanuel steadfastly refused to tell the lie, Norton tied his wrists to a barn rafter and hoisted him up until only Emmanuel's toes touched the floor. For the next two hours Norton flogged the boy with switches. Still the lad refused to tell the lie. When Emmanuel was let down, he turned to Norton and said, "Pa, I'm so cold."

That night Emmanuel Dannan died. He died believing it wrong to tell a lie.

Children shame us at times. Their beauty sometimes brings to light the ugliness of some of us adults. Studying human nature, one isn't surprised that the Carpenter took a little child, set him in the midst of the crowd, and told listeners that to enter the kingdom of heaven they would have to become like that child.

I have been shamed and humbled many times by the honesty and humility of children. We adults have many prejudices ingrained in us over the years. Children are often free of these prejudices. I heard a fellow say once that the races should be separated among the little children because "they didn't know the difference." As the song says, you have to be taught to hate.

Maybe one day adults will resume their belief in some

of those great virtues they embraced as children—freedom, brotherhood, justice, love, helpfulness, kindness. Our world desperately needs them.

One of the best investments we as adults can make in life is the shaping of a young mind toward that which is true in life. Parents and teachers and counselors who spend their time teaching a child to love do far more in preventing the destruction of the world than all the ruling bodies.

Emmanuel Dannan was a great man, even if he was just eight years old. He remained true to the highest values he knew. After his death, a fund was begun to erect a monument to the boy who would not tell a lie. A total of $1,099 was given, but the treasurer took every penny of it. That was in 1851. In 1954, 103 years later, funds were solicited once again, and a monument was erected in Emmanuel Dannan's honor.

The Nazarene once said, "Happy are those who suffer persecution because they do what God requires; the kingdom of heaven belongs to them." I believe I know where Emmanuel lives now. In that place that belongs to him.

THE STORY OF JOHNNY RING

"For this is the will of God, that by doing good you may put to silence the ignorance of foolish men." (1 Peter 2:15)

You've probably never heard of Johnny Ring. Johnny isn't very famous. He did little that our world considers worthy of fame. Nevertheless, the story of Johnny Ring deserves to be passed on.

Johnny lived during the War Between the States. When a company of soldiers was being organized in the area in which Johnny lived, he asked to be a part of it. But the captain had other thoughts. In his thinking Johnny was too young and too little. The captain refused to take the boy into his group.

But Johnny was determined. If he couldn't be a soldier, he would be a soldier's helper. He asked to go along as the servant of the captain. Following some discussion, the captain agreed. He admired the boy's drive. "You'll be a better soldier if I can help take care of some of your things," Johnny had said.

Johnny was a good servant. He kept the captain's boots polished, his tent neat, and his sword shining. But while Johnny was a good servant, he wasn't always obedient. You see, Johnny had promised his mother before she died that he would read the Bible every night. This didn't set well with the captain, who was an avowed atheist. Johnny would read his Bible in the captain's tent each night before he went to bed. One night the captain ordered Johnny never to read the Bible in his tent again. Yet Johnny continued his Bible study, often reading while the captain wasn't in the tent.

The troops under the command of the captain were surprised by the enemy one day and forced to retreat across a bridge. To keep them from counterattacking, the Confederate forces set the bridge on fire. Suddenly, in the midst of battle, Johnny Ring was seen running across the burning bridge. Soldiers on both sides held their fire. Shortly thereafter, the bridge engulfed in flames, they watched as Johnny Ring ran back across—carrying his captain's prized sword in his hands. As Johnny reached the other side, he fell to the ground with his clothes on fire. Some of the soldiers managed to extinguish the fire, but it wasn't long before Johnny Ring was dead.

After Johnny was buried, the captain began to think seriously about Johnny and his Christian faith. Maybe the faith that Johnny had would help him be like Johnny. It wasn't long till the captain embraced the faith of Johnny and claimed the Carpenter of Galilee as his Master.

Nearly fifteen years later he became a Baptist minister. During his ministry, he founded Temple University and the Temple University Medical Center. All told, he raised

$11 million for Christian causes. More than once, when questioned about his long hours of work, he would say, "I have to live two lives—mine and Johnny Ring's. Johnny died for me."

Like we said, you probably never heard of Johnny Ring. He is a hero nonetheless.

PAY THE PRICE OR FORGET THE CAUSE

"Whoever desires to come after Me, let him deny himself, and take up his cross, and follow Me." (Mark 8:34)

Gerard LePage was a pacifist. Of thousands who claim that title, he was one of the few fit to wear it.

LePage, a Specialist 5 from Waterbury, Connecticut, was arrested by military police shortly after attending a midnight Christmas service. The MPs didn't have to do that, because LePage was on his way to turn himself in.

LePage served ten months as a clerk in Vietnam and would have been eligible for an honorable discharge in a couple of months. He told news reporters he would be a hypocrite if he continued to serve in the military.

He had said earlier that he would remain AWOL at least thirty days, long enough to be classified a deserter. Then he would turn himself in. At the Christmas service LePage read a statement, saying, "This sanctuary is just the beginning. The commitment to love and freedom and life will endure." Four hours after the service, MP vehicles stopped the car in which LePage was riding, and he was arrested.

LePage could have used underground connections to get to Canada, as did thousands of others. But LePage didn't want to do that. "Going to Canada is a cop-out," he said. And he was right.

Here's the reason this man gained my admiration. "It's my right to speak out and then take the punishment for it," he said. That's a sign of bigness in a person—to oppose something he or she believes is wrong and then to be willing to pay the penalty for that opposition. LePage asked no favors. He knew the punishment for desertion. But he believed something, believed it enough to pay the price of punishment. That, I admire.

There was another man some two thousand years ago who was equally courageous. There was wrong in society, He said, and He set out to correct it. He walked the hillsides of the little province of Galilee, teaching people a new way of living, a new way of worshiping, a new way of serving. He went from Jerusalem to Jericho to Sidon, teaching those who would listen about a new way of life.

And when it came time for Him to face the authorities concerning this new way of life He preached, He did so fully prepared to pay the penalty. And so the powers that were took His life on a Judean hillside, hanging Him on a cross between two thieves.

I admire someone who stands up for what he or she believes to be right and then is willing to take the punishment for that belief. I have nothing but disgust for that person who knowingly breaks the law and then tries to escape the consequences. While they both do the same thing, there is a world of difference in their methods, their reasons, and their characters.

If there is an unjust law, and you feel you must break it, first make up your mind that you will pay the penalty for breaking it. If you aren't willing to pay the penalty, forget it. You do the cause more harm than good. It is a small person who wants the glory without the cross.

FINDING OUR PLACE IN LIFE

"Now you are the body of Christ, and members individually." (1 Corinthians 12:27)

Some years ago there was a young Canadian man who wanted to find a place to serve others. Searching, praying, looking, he came to the conclusion that God had called him to be a minister, so he began his preparation. He worked hard to become a minister, but things just didn't seem to fall into place.

Following a trying period, he finally left the ministry and turned to medicine, studying at the University of Toronto. During World War I he served his country as a soldier. Returning to Canada, he practiced medicine in London, Ontario. But business wasn't too good. Few patients visited his practice.

But he didn't become discouraged. A man of resourcefulness, he began reading all the latest medical journals in his spare time. He became obsessed with the tragedies he saw resulting from the disease called diabetes. It was taking the lives of many people. In 1921 he gave up his medical practice and borrowed a laboratory in which to conduct experiments.

This man had little help or encouragement from his friends. Nevertheless, he worked steadily in the laboratory. He was searching for a cure for the dreaded disease of diabetes. He had a helper by the name of Charles Best. Both applied their knowledge and skill to finding a cure.

Sometimes it's hard to find one's place in life. Sometimes it seems that we just don't fit in anywhere. We try one thing and it doesn't work out. Then we go to another field with little success. There is a feeling in all of us—and I think it is divinely implanted—that somewhere there is work for us to do. And there is!

We all have a role to play in the theater of life. None of us are of so little importance that we should be left out when the curtain is raised and the drama begins. We each have a special talent given to us by our Creator, one He expects us to use in service to our fellow human beings. We probably aren't able to do some things as well as other people do them. But then they aren't capable of doing some things as well as we do them, either. We should each do the best we can with what we have. The Bible calls that *stewardship*.

If we earnestly search, we will find our place in life. How was it that the Good Shepherd said it? "Seek, and you shall find." I believe He meant that. Keep looking, keep searching, keep hunting for your "place." One day you'll find it. And life will have meaning and purpose, because you do.

The man who left the ministry for medicine was Sir

Frederick Grant Banting. He found his place in medical research and discovered insulin. Millions of diabetics are glad he did. If you haven't found your place, keep searching. You will.

PART VIII

THE CARPENTER TEACHES FAITH

LIFE ISN'T EASY

"Because narrow is the gate and difficult is the way which leads to life, and there are few who find it." (Matthew 7:14)

We learn early that life isn't easy. From the moment a baby leaves the security of its mother's body, it begins to cry. And from that moment on, life never lets up.

There are two attitudes one can take toward life. One is the "take care of myself, don't bother with the other person, don't get too involved" attitude. This is by far the most common, for the simple reason that it places no demands on us. We can do as we please. We can just live out our lives, pat ourselves on the back, tell ourselves we're doing all we should be doing.

There is another attitude toward life. Those who hold this attitude view life as a sacred trust, one given to us by the eternal Father for the benefit of Him and for each other. Few are willing to adopt this attitude. It places demands on us that we don't want and causes us to strive for goals the masses call impossible. This is often a lonely way of life.

Often we're tempted to give up, to call it quits, to say that it's impossible to attain that high calling. We're tempted to lower our goals and think more about ourselves.

But then we ultimately come back to this: Life isn't supposed to be easy. It is supposed to be a challenge. And the moment we cease working toward a high calling, we begin to deteriorate into nothing but a self-satisfied, selfish human in the "I-don't-care" crowd.

When we're ready to throw in the towel and call it quits, what we really need is assurance that what we're doing has some significance and lasting value. For as long as we can believe that what we're doing has God's stamp of approval, we can surmount any obstacle that stands before us. But once we stop believing in that high calling, we're doomed to a life of selfishness.

Sometimes the night gets dark. And we begin to question whether we should forget that calling. Our work becomes difficult, and we see little chance that it will get easier in the future. In times like that, the only thing that will sustain us is the knowledge that what we're doing has God's approval, that our efforts will not be in vain, and that our God will gladly pour out His grace on those who need it.

Life is easy only when we are selfish. It's hard when we choose the high road. And while it gets to be awful dark sometimes on the high road, we need to remember that daylight always follows darkness.

WHY DID HE COME?

"I must preach the kingdom of God to the other cities also, because for this purpose I have been sent." (Luke 4:43)

Iwant to dispute something you've heard all your life about the Galilean. And I want to do it in such a manner that you cannot possibly misunderstand me. I wish to make myself explicitly clear on the subject. I don't want you to think there is a misprint or that I don't mean what I say.

Now, with that as a foundation, brace yourself for the statement I'm about to make: The Galilean didn't come to get us into heaven. There, I've said it.

I know what you've heard all your life. I know what you've been led to believe. I know what some well-intentioned folks have spent a lot of time trying to tell you. But I still want you to know that this much is true: Jesus didn't come to get us into heaven.

I had *heard* that this was the reason He came. I had heard that all my life. Everybody on the radio, in the pulpit, or at my door has been telling me this was the reason He came—to get me into heaven.

In growing up, I read it in some literature. As an adult, I continue to read it. Some have made an extensive search and even listed the things I have to do if I want to go there. Unless I do these things, they say, I can never make it to heaven. Despite what they've written, despite what they've said, I still want to make one thing clear: Jesus didn't come to get us into heaven.

I know, I know. Some of you will write me. I will receive bundles of letters refuting what I've said. Letters that will tell me the rules I have to follow, the steps I have to take. They will be filled with biblical quotes. But even if I get a thousand letters it won't change the truth.

You see, there is one fact that we always overlook. That is that we cannot get into heaven unless heaven first gets into us. And that's the reason He came, to get heaven into us!

HE'S THERE TOO

"Surely the LORD is in this place, and I did not know it." (Genesis 28:16)

Sam put on his coat, picked up his briefcase, and walked to the door. Saying good-bye to the rest of the family, he proceeded to his car. He backed out of the driveway and headed down the road to his office. At the intersection he looked both ways and then started across. That's when it happened.

There was a terrible screech of tires sliding on the pavement as an oncoming vehicle tried to come to a sudden stop. Sam looked to his right to see a big tractor-trailer bearing down on him. His instinct told him to brace himself, to prepare for a terrible accident. The truck was about to crash into his small car. He clenched the wheel and waited. But, miraculously, the driver of the truck managed to get the rig stopped just before the anticipated collision.

With a sigh of relief, Sam uttered a quick prayer of thanks. Now Sam wasn't normally a religious man. He lived mostly by his own creeds and had little interest in "kid stuff" like prayers. But for some reason, he let it slip. "Thank You, Lord," he said.

Sam and the driver of the truck got out and surveyed the situation. "Man," said the truck driver, "you're a mighty lucky person. Just a split-second difference in timing and you probably wouldn't be around right now. You'd better be glad I had my brakes reworked last week. I'd hate to think what would have happened if I hadn't. Buddy, you'd better thank goodness you're still alive."

"Mister," said Sam, "I already have."

In a few moments Sam was once again on his way to the office. At a service station along the route he took he saw Bill, a friend of his who worked in the same office. Bill was also the "religious" guy in their group. He was a regular churchgoer. Sam wheeled in to speak to Bill and tell him about the truck.

"Hey, Bill," Sam yelled out his window as he pulled alongside his friend. "God is really taking care of me this morning. I pulled out in front of this big truck, but He performed a miracle and stopped it just before it got to me. It sure is great how the Lord takes care of us, isn't it?"

"It sure is," said Bill. "He performed a miracle for me this morning too."

"He did?" Sam asked excitedly. "What happened? Did you nearly get hit by a big truck too?"

"No," said Bill. "He just kept me from pulling in front of any."

Strange how we can find Him in the "miracles" and not in the everyday events, isn't it?

THE GAME WE DIDN'T WIN

"Gather My saints together to Me."
(Psalm 50:5)

I was thinking about some old times the other day. I remember quite clearly a high school football game. It was a very important game for our team. We had gone through nearly the entire season undefeated and untied, and it looked as if we were en route to a perfect season. We had a big game coming up that would decide the conference championship. If we could win this one, the championship was all ours.

There was much excitement about that game. We played on our opponent's field, but nearly everyone from our hometown had followed us over, and the stands were packed with fans. We felt certain we could defeat our opponent because we had beaten by twenty-six points a team that had previously beaten them by thirteen.

But once the game got under way, nothing seemed to go right for us. We could move the ball down to the opponent's five-yard line, but we never got any farther. We spent fifty percent of the first half inside our opponent's five. But for some reason we could never get the ball into the end zone.

Late in the half, the other team intercepted a pass and ran nearly the length of the field for a touchdown. The extra point was good, and at the half we went into the dressing room trailing 7-0. Ours was a rather dejected group, for we hadn't been behind in a game all season. Most of the players were already conceding defeat. I remember that one other player and myself were still positive, still convinced we could win.

In the second half we played a little better. We managed to score a touchdown. And when it came time to call a play for that crucial extra point, the coach called an option play, a play in which the quarterback could either elect to run with the ball or pitch it to the halfback—me. Well, at the last minute he pitched it out. I grabbed that ball, and I don't believe a bulldozer could have stopped me. The score was 7-7, with time left to score again.

I played extremely hard in those last few minutes, and once I nearly broke away. We were so close to scoring, but I didn't have the necessary speed or coordination, and my try was short. I remember walking off the field when the game was over, feeling awfully despondent. In my book, a tie was as bad as a loss. As I walked off the field, my father was waiting for me on the sidelines. He had never done that before. But I can remember the expression on his face. He was proud of me, and proud of the game I'd played, despite the tie.

I've come to realize over the years that my heavenly Father is like that also. He's proud of us when we've done our best, even if it wasn't good enough. Every time I lose or tie now, after doing my best, I remember that. And, somehow, it gives me strength to try again.

DOUBTING THE POWER
OF GOD'S LOVE

"Jesus answered and said to them, 'You are mistaken, not knowing the Scriptures nor the power of God.'" (Matthew 22:29)

There was a lady who came to the United States a while back. Her coming caused quite a stir. Some welcomed her and some cursed her upon her arrival. But regardless of what people thought about her, she set her mind to come to this country and did so.

She had to slip away from her native country. Had the authorities there known she was planning on coming here they would have certainly put a stop to it. And her coming greatly endangered the family and friends she left behind.

This lady differed from most immigrants in several ways. First, she was a member of the aristocracy of the country she left behind. And she had, according to its standards, a good life where she was. Also, she left behind a son, twenty-one, and a daughter, fifteen.

This lady left her country because of her religious beliefs. She came seeking "freedom of expression" for herself. "When I became a grown-up," she said, "I found it impossible to exist without God in my heart. Instead of struggling and causing unnecessary bloodshed,people must work together for the progress of humanity. . . . There are no capitalists or communists for me. There are good people and bad, honest and dishonest."

Go back and read again what she said. "When I became a grown-up, I found it impossible to exist without God in my heart." Maybe our trouble is that we've never "grown up." Oh, we may be six feet tall physically but still have failed to grow up. Some of the most childish people are giants physically.

Notice, too, that she had a solution to the world's problems. "People must work together for the progress of humanity." Another man once said that we should "love one another." I wonder if this isn't what the lady with the new country was saying.

She goes on to say that people are "good and bad, honest and dishonest." Let us give thanks for someone who can still see good and bad and isn't confused by all the gray matter.

In case you're wondering about the power of the Creator's love, wonder no more. The lady we have written about is proof positive that He still works in this struggling world. For if He can reach this lady, He can reach anyone.

The lady's name was Svetlana Alliluyeva. If that doesn't ring a bell with you, you might know her as the daughter and only surviving child of Joseph Stalin, one of the most bloodthirsty tyrants the world has ever known.

PART IX

FOLLOWING THE CARPENTER MEANS LIVING BY THE TRUTH

CROSSING RIVERS

"Therefore do not worry about tomorrow, for tomorrow will worry about its own things. Sufficient for the day is its own trouble."
(Matthew 6:34)

Abraham Lincoln and some of his friends were once forced to do some traveling during a very rainy season. They had crossed many small streams, and the water was high and fast in all of them. After a long day of battling currents that had nearly washed them away, they came to a lodge where they spent the night.

Warming themselves by the fire that night, the men talked about how high the streams were and how fast the water was flowing. Then someone mentioned the fact that the next day the group would be forced to cross Fox River. Fox River was difficult to cross even when the water was low, and if it was up in comparison to the other streams, it would be nearly impossible to cross.

As they sat around and talked, many expressed the worry that Fox River would be impassable. Because they had an appointment to keep, it was important to the group that they not be delayed on their journey.

For some time that night the group sat around discussing Fox River and the danger that would face them when the time came to cross it. Following some discussion, someone noticed that there was at the lodge a Methodist preacher who traveled the territory quite often and was familiar with Fox River.

"Preacher, you've been listening to us talk about that river. Do you have any special way of getting across it? Any rules to follow that might help us?" a member of the group asked.

"Well, now that you asked," replied the preacher, "I do have one fixed rule about Fox River. I've crossed it many times, and I know it's a problem to get across sometimes. But I've solved the problem with just one rule."

"What's your secret, Preacher? Have you got a special place to cross?" they asked.

"Nope, haven't got a special place to cross. I cross it where everyone else does," he said.

"Then you must have a float put back nearby to help you cross it," one of the group surmised.

"Nope, haven't got a float put back. Just never did have the time to build one or the money to buy one," said the preacher.

"But you said you had a rule about crossing that river!" one man said irritably. "If you haven't got a special place to cross, or a float to cross on, then tell us what your rule about crossing the river is."

"Well, sir," said the preacher, "I've crossed Fox River

many times. But I've learned never to cross it till I reach it." And with that he rolled over and went to sleep.

It's a pretty good rule to follow.

IT'S WHERE YOU ARE

"He who heeds the word wisely will find good, / And whoever trusts in the LORD, happy is he."
(Proverbs 16:20)

Some time ago I heard about a man in Phoenix who had rented an apartment but couldn't move into it because he had lost it! Actually, he couldn't find it. It seems that he had sold his photofinishing business in Appleton, Wisconsin, and moved to Phoenix. Upon his arrival in the city, he checked into a hotel. That same day he found an apartment and paid a month's rent in advance. But he drove away without noting the address.

After fourteen hours of driving around the city to locate the apartment, he notified a local newspaper of his plight. A reporter wrote an article about it, and the fellow who had rented him the apartment read the article and called him at the hotel. It seems that the apartment was just two blocks, a couple of minutes, away from the hotel!

Then there was the case of the ophthalmologist in Toronto, Ontario. This doctor was punched in the eye and, as a result, lost one of his contact lenses. Unable to find the lens, he was fitted for another shortly thereafter. But his injured eye kept discharging, and his new lens kept popping out. It should have. You see, the lens the doctor had searched for but couldn't find had been pushed into his eyelid, where it remained unnoticed.

As a student, I worked in a grocery store to help defray my expenses. As I was stocking the shelves one day, a man kept walking up and down the aisle looking for some product. Finally he stopped in the section where the product should be. After continuing to look for quite a while, he asked me if I knew where it was located. Reaching to the spot where he had been looking, I picked up the product and gave it to him.

"If it had been a snake it would have bitten me!" he exclaimed.

Not long after that, I began a search early one morning for my glasses. After searching for several minutes and failing to find them, I accused the children of misplacing them.

Seeing that I was about to lose what little temper I had, Lynda started searching with me. She came into the room where I was frantically hunting and started to speak, only to have a wide grin come across her face.

"Go look in a mirror," she said.

I took the hint and suddenly realized that I was wearing the glasses I had been so desperately hunting!

Isn't it funny sometimes how we can search high and low for something, and then end up finding it in a place where it should have been so simple to find?

Now there is a truth here that could be applied to countless realms. But for the sake of simplicity, let's try just one: happiness. It's right where you are. All you have to do is find it.

MORALITY VERSUS ECONOMICS

"For the love of money is a root of all kinds of evil, for which some have strayed from the faith in their greediness, and pierced themselves through with many sorrows." (1 Timothy 6:10)

Don't give up on people! There's still goodness left in some of them. Mrs. Jean Cardon of Los Angeles is proof of that. Mrs. Cardon was walking down a sidewalk one day when she found a

$100 bill on the street. She carried it to the police station and turned it over to the authorities.

"So, what's so great about that?" you ask. Well, I would agree that there are quite a few people who would do likewise. But Mrs. Cardon was something of a special case in my book. Why? For the simple reason that at the time she found the money she didn't have enough change for a bus ticket to the police station. In fact, she was flat broke. So she walked ten blocks to turn the money in. And to top it all off, she didn't have a job at the time.

Why did she do it? "I just followed my impulse," she said. Her "impulse" told her that turning the money in was the right thing to do. "Some people tell me I was foolish," she added.

Well, you could have predicted that. There are always some who call honesty foolishness. To them it would be a simple case of finders keepers, losers weepers.

After turning in the money Mrs. Cardon opened her first savings account in twenty years with a deposit of $700. No, she didn't get a reward for turning in the money. It seems that people heard of her good deed and wanted to help a person with such high morals.

There is within each of us that "impulse" Mrs. Cardon spoke of. Unless, of course, we have killed it with neglect. It's there to help us make the right decision. Did you notice that Mrs. Cardon said that her impulse told her it was the right thing to do? That's one reason that impulse is there, to help us determine right from wrong.

For Mrs. Cardon it was a moral decision, not an

economic one, that was called for. Money was involved here, but it was no basis for a decision. The only basis for a decision was what was right. Do you think that perhaps the business world could take a tip here? Many times there is a moral decision that overrides the economic one. And maybe there is a hint for you and me here too—to spend our money like we should, with an obligation to do right. If we could follow Mrs. Cardon's example, maybe we could change the fact that as a nation we spend twice as much on alcohol as we do on the Carpenter's work.

Admittedly, money—too much or too little—creates all kinds of problems for most of us. And we're often tempted to stretch our morals a little to cover our economics. But is it the money itself that creates the problem? Or is it greed?

If you should decide to take the tip and make the change in regard to money and economics, remember Mrs. Cardon's experience. Some people will call you foolish.

WHAT IS FREEDOM?

"Now the Lord is the Spirit; and where the Spirit of the Lord is, there is liberty."
(2 Corinthians 3:17)

Freedom. Millions are in search of it. They want what our Constitution guarantees them. Freedom of speech, freedom of expression, freedom of the press. And they are seizing these rights, these freedoms, because they are tired of being enslaved.

Have you ever pondered this word *freedom*? What do we mean by it? How does one explain freedom? Just what does it mean to be free? Our country is full of people who have, they think, found the definition of the word. Tired of all the old restraints and restrictions, they are exercising their freedom. They fill the newsstands and magazine racks with pornography because they have "freedom of the press," a right guaranteed by the Constitution. They are on the warpath to get any mention of a higher power out of our schools, because "freedom of religion" guarantees them this right. And the list could go on.

Nearly two thousand years ago a lowly Nazarene Carpenter told a story about people like these modern-day searchers for freedom. This Nazarene said there was a young man who came to his father and demanded his share of the estate while he was young enough to enjoy it. The father granted his son's wish.

Soon the young man had packed his bags and headed for another country. He was tired of all the old restraints and restrictions of his society. He was tired of people telling him that he couldn't do what he wanted to do. He wanted freedom! And as he walked down that dusty road away from the father he felt this freedom in his soul. He was free at last, free to do as he pleased! Finally, he'd found what he had wanted all his life—freedom!

But the Carpenter didn't end the story there. He said that before long the young man's money was gone, and with it went his freedom. He had to go to work in order to survive. The best job he could get was feeding pigs.

Finally, amid the filth of the pigpens, the young man came to his senses. He went home to seek his father's permission to work as one of the hired hands on the family farm. He was willing to take the lowest place on his father's farm rather than continue to "enjoy" his new-found "freedom."

What is freedom? Well, never make the mistake of thinking that freedom is a matter of rights. It isn't. It's a matter of responsibility. And no one can become free until he has become a slave to something higher and greater than himself.

Freedom. I hope that those who are crying out the loudest for the freedom to do as they please will one day, like the prodigal son, come to their senses. For the more they get of what they want, the less they will want of what they get.

"Make us captives, Lord, and then we shall be free."

INTEGRITY

"He who walks with integrity walks securely, / But he who perverts his ways will become known." (Proverbs 10:9)

During the Korean War, an American general by the name of Dean was captured by the communists. In the Korean town Chong-ju, General Dean was told by the communists that he had a few minutes in which to write a farewell note to his family. General Dean figured that he had thirty minutes at the most before he would be taken out and shot.

In such a situation, no one would waste words. General Dean didn't, either. In his letter to his family, he wrote only one sentence, but it revealed the whole of his character. The sentence was directed to General Dean's son. Here's what he wrote: "Tell Bill the word is *integrity*."

Not popularity, or success, or fame, or happiness, but integrity. How desperately our world needs that.

To have integrity is to be true to one's self and to one's Maker. To have integrity is to put truth above all else. It is to be unwilling to sell one's soul for a few dollars or a cheap thrill.

A person can afford to lose position, income, prestige. These things are dispensable: They can be replaced. But not integrity. A person can live with truth, though it be difficult and trying. But no one can live with a lie and remain a person of integrity.

We are tempted today to compromise our values, to call a little wrong nearly right. But we can't do that without losing the thing that's most important to us: Our integrity. We must stand for the truth, even if it means the loss of a job or prestige, or scorn and rejection by our contemporaries.

"Tell Bill the word is *integrity*." Yes, that is the word. How much we need to hear it, believe it, live by it. Not success. Not popularity. Not position. But integrity! The word means uprightness. That's the way the Creator intended that mankind should walk—uprightly. Not only in a physical sense but in a spiritual and moral sense. We are not only to live with truth, but we are to live by it.

What the world needs today is not more people of wealth, or even more of those with wisdom. What the world needs today is more people of integrity, people who are willing to plant their feet solidly on the truth and refuse to budge when faced by the temptations of the world. Yes, we need people of character, people who will not compromise truth.

The word is *integrity*. Please pass the word.

SALTY

"And I thank Christ Jesus our Lord who has enabled me." (1 Timothy 1:12)

A long time ago I heard the story of Salty the dog. Salty was a twenty-one-month-old mongrel. An average dog, but a determined dog, nevertheless.

Salty belonged to a woman in Detroit. She kept Salty for some time and then gave her to some friends in the suburbs, because, she said, "My place is so small I thought it wasn't fair to keep her here."

The new owners kept Salty until she gave birth to a litter of puppies, then they gave her to a family in Cheboygan, 272 miles northwest of Detroit.

One day, Salty disappeared. For the next two weeks she traveled—over 272 miles of woods, fields, streams, roads, and towns she'd never seen before. And although

Salty didn't know how she was going to get there, she knew where she wanted to go—home. Back to Detroit.

On New Year's Day, her first owner went downstairs to take out the trash and there stood Salty!

"She knocked me down and started licking my face and kissing me," the woman reported. "She was wet and tired and so dirty that it was difficult to tell what color she was. Her paws were bleeding, and she was starving." But with tail wagging, Salty was home at last. Her journey was over.

Salty set out for something she wanted more than anything in the world. And she got it. Now, this is a story about a dog, but if you will raise the level just slightly, you will find the same truth about humans. For we humans, like Salty the dog, usually get to the place in life we want to go. The reason many of us never get farther than we do is simple: We never really want to get any farther.

I recall the story of one man who set out to accomplish something in life, something He wanted more than anything else. And the road that led to His dreams wasn't an easy one, either. But He was intent on his course. Through towns where He wasn't wanted, over roads where He was spit upon, through valleys that echoed with hatred that the "good" people had for Him—He traveled on.

When He finally arrived at his destination, when He'd accomplished the thing He'd set out to accomplish, He was bloody, bruised, and weak from a merciless flogging. In His hands were huge holes, caused by spikes with which He was suspended on the cross. But He wasn't beaten.

While Salty came home dirty, tired, bloody, and shaggy, she got what she wanted—to see her master again. The Carpenter from Galilee accomplished His goal too. To make it possible for us to see our Master again.

And because of His journey, our journey is over.

PART X

THE CARPENTER
GIVES HOPE

IF YOU CAN'T SING, WHITTLE!

"There are diversities of gifts, but the same Spirit." (1 Corinthians 12:4)

He was a lad in the town of Cremona, Italy, in the middle of the seventeenth century. Cremona was a musical town, and great acclaim was given to those who could sing or play an instrument. Wanting to be accepted and given some recognition, he tried singing. But his friends called him "squeaky voice," and he soon realized that his singing would never gain him the acclaim he sought.

The lad then tried to learn to play an instrument, but his success at that wasn't much better than at singing. So he was a dejected boy as he walked through the streets of Cremona with his friends and listened to their beautiful voices. About the only thing he could do was whittle.

One day he was sitting on the sidewalk whittling as three of his friends played and sang beautiful songs for the people passing by. Appreciating the musical ability of the young men, many people dropped coins into their hands to reward their efforts. One man stopped longer than the others and even asked the boys to sing a song again. After they finished, he dropped a coin into the hand of one singer. Then he moved on down the street.

Upon looking, the boys discovered that it was a gold coin! It was quite a lot of money to give a street singer.

"Who was he?" asked the boy who whittled.

"It was Amati," his friend with the beautiful voice replied.

"Amati who?" asked the lad.

"Nicolo Amati," the friend replied. "He is the greatest violin maker in all of Italy."

That evening at home, the lad thought about the man named Nicolo Amati. He was a man who had succeeded in the musical field. But he neither sang nor played. The more he thought about the violin maker, the more he became convinced that he wanted to become a violin maker too. He wanted to become the best violin maker in Italy!

Early the next morning the lad hurried off to the home of Nicolo Amati. He sat on the doorstep after arriving and waited for the great violin maker to come out. When Amati appeared, the lad told him that he wanted to become a violin maker and asked Amati if he would teach him to make violins. He explained to Amati that he couldn't sing or play, but that he could whittle. And more than anything else, he wanted to make violins.

Amati accepted the youth as a pupil. Day after day, week after week, month after month, year after year the young man studied from the master. In due time, his work became known in Cremona, then in Italy, and finally, throughout the whole world.

We may not have the talent to do some things as well as other people. But God has given each of us a special talent that, if developed, can help us help others. Antonio Stradivari found this to be true. To this very day people pay large sums of money to play a Stradivarius violin.

Just because you can't sing or play doesn't mean you can't make music.

PERSISTENCE

"Let us run with endurance the race that is set before us." (Hebrews 12:1)

There is a story told about a certain little boy who wanted a watch. Day in and day out he pestered his parents to get him one. His parents put him off every way they could. Finally they were driven to the breaking point. His father told the youngster that he didn't want to hear another word about a watch.

For the rest of that week the lad said nothing about a watch. He knew that to do so would certainly bring some discomfort to his behind. Sunday soon rolled around and the family was gathered together for a period of devotion. It was a custom in the family for each member to learn a new verse of Scripture and to recite it each Sunday during devotions.

Every other member of the family had said their Scripture verse when it came time for the youngster to recite his. Looking up with a solemn face, he quoted his verse perfectly: "What I say unto you I say unto all: watch!" Well, I'm not certain if he got his watch or a spanking, but one thing I can say for him: He was persistent.

And that's a quality all of us could use—persistence. For one of our faults today is that we give up too soon, call it quits after a single setback, let failure break us instead of make us.

There is little a person cannot do in this life if he or she sets out to do it and stays with it. One reason we don't accomplish more is that we are quick quitters. We experience a setback or two and then we say it can't be done. We give up. But history is full of things that "couldn't be done." And that means it's also full of people who did them.

The world looks up in admiration to those who have staying power. They don't have to have great brains or great riches or vast opportunities. But if they believe in something and have the persistence to stay with that belief regardless of the praise or scorn they receive, the world ultimately will look up to them.

One reason there aren't more people with persistence is the simple reason that it takes a big person to stick with the ship when the waves get high. It's easier to get into a lifeboat and float to safety. But the person with persistence is seeking neither safety nor an easier mission. He has something he wants to do, and he believes he can do it. So he stays with it, come what may. Then one day, the "impossible" has been accomplished.

Great goals aren't easy to accomplish. They require great people to accomplish them. And great people are people who keep on keeping on. I believe God wants a person who says, "I can." I believe God wants a person who will try again.

"All things are possible . . ." He is waiting to see if you believe Him. If you do, try again.

WORRY

"But I am like a green olive tree in the house of God; / I trust in the mercy of God forever and ever." (Psalm 52:8)

Some years ago a preacher was sitting alone in his study late at night, desperately worried about a difficult problem. Along about midnight God came to him and said, "You go to bed. I'll sit up the rest of the night." So he took God at His word and went to bed. And God sat up the rest of that night.

Worry has never helped a single person. It has hurt many. One man remarked once that he had worried about a lot of things in his life, and that most of them never came to pass. All the energy he spent worrying was wasted.

Now, there's a difference between worry and concern. We *are* to be concerned, to care. But worry is undue and unnecessary, and it taxes our mental health. Maybe God is trying to say something to us by leaving the word completely out of His book.

Somewhere along life's way, it is of great advantage to us to turn life's problems over to the Creator. For it is too difficult a road to navigate alone. Life hands out some big burdens, and too many of them can weigh us down.

The Galilean offered this invitation: "Come to Me, all who labor and are heavy laden, and I will give you rest. Take My yoke upon you, and learn from Me; for I am gentle and lowly in heart, and you will find rest for your souls. For My yoke is easy and My burden is light."

There are some things in life that we need to turn over to the Maker of life. All our worrying will not help matters one iota; it will just sap our strength and deform our personality. Worry, negative thinking, has nothing to give us.

Most of us are weighted down by some burden now and then. Life has a way of handing out to some pretty tough loads. Life isn't easy. It wasn't intended to be. But neither was it intended that we worry.

Our God has promised that He will give us rest. It

seems not only foolish but also blasphemy to reject His promise. Yet we worry about things that have already happened, or about things over which we have absolutely no control, or about things that *might* happen. Most of the things we worry about will never happen!

There comes a time in our concern, often in the midnight of our concern, when we need to turn our problems over to God. Then we should go to bed, and let God sit up the rest of the night.

You can be certain of one thing—He will.

COMING OUT OF HIDING

"Then the LORD God called to Adam and said to him, 'Where are you?'" (Genesis 3:9)

In 1953, government authorities found a Japanese soldier hiding in the Philippine jungles. The soldier, who had been hiding there for nine years, was unaware that World War II was over. He wasted nine years of his life, foolishly hiding in the jungles.

As strange as that story may seem, it has a parallel in our society. Countless individuals are hiding, they think, from God. We're like the first man, Adam. We know we have sinned against Him, so we try to hide. Sometimes we hide behind our work. (We work on Sunday, or so hard during the week.) Sometimes we hide behind the faults of others. ("Joe is a Christian and look at *him*.") Sometimes we hide behind our independence. ("I don't need God.")

But we don't have to hide anymore. God is not a God whom we have to hide from when we have sinned. He is a God who will forgive if we will only ask Him with a devout heart. This is one of the greatest truths that the Galilean ever proclaimed. Remember the prodigal son, who sinned against his father? Remember how the father loved him and ran to meet him? Well, God is like that.

God is searching for us because He loves us. That was the reason for the Cross, the tomb, and the Resurrection. He was trying to bring all people to Him. We cannot, no matter how hard we try, hide from Him. Adam tried to hide, and even though we're told God asked where he was, God knew. Adam couldn't hide. Neither can we. We can ignore Him, or disregard Him, or even run from Him. But we cannot escape Him.

The soldier in the Philippine jungles was living under the false assumption that if he was found, some terrible and lasting punishment would befall him. For that reason he dared not come out of hiding. There are those who are fleeing from God, hiding from Him, because they believe some terrible and lasting punishment awaits them. The soldier found that those whom he thought to be his enemies had become his friends. That's what repentant humans find about God. Expecting punishment, they find forgiveness when they ask for it.

It's a shame for a person to waste so much of life hiding on an island. It's a greater tragedy for us to waste so much of our lives hiding from God. "Eye hath not seen, nor ear heard, nor the heart of man conceived, what God has prepared for those who love Him," said the little Jewish tentmaker. And it's true. Every word of it. Even the Master Himself proclaimed, "I have come that you may have life and have it more abundantly."

Why did the soldier remain hidden all those years? Because he made no attempt to discover the facts. Why do so many of us hide from God? For the simple reason that we have made no attempt to discover the truth about the love of God. Hiding from God, we wind up losing everything He has in store for us.

The greatest injustice that we could do ourselves would be to continue hiding and fail to seek the love of God that awaits us.

DID YOU EVER WANT TO QUIT?

"Then Jesus said to them, 'Follow Me, and I will make you become fishers of men.' They immediately left their nets and followed Him." (Mark 1:17–18)

Did you ever want to quit? Did you ever want to "hang 'em up" and call it a game? If you haven't, then you aren't normal. Every normal person has periods when he or she is ready to throw in the towel.

Several years ago I charted a course for my life. I chose what I believed to be the highest and truest way of living. I gave myself to it. And I have pursued it. But there have been times when I've wanted to quit, to call it a game and hang up the togs.

Quitting is tempting because it's easier. When you get knocked down over and over it's hard to get up and go another time. When it seems as though you're behind and can never catch up, it's hard to keep trying.

Life is tremendously demanding if a person pledges himself to the best he knows. It becomes so difficult sometimes that the temptation to give up is strong. The benefits of giving up can seem appealing.

I can understand why some people have given up. They grew tired of following their highest dream. Then they started demanding less and less of themselves. Finally, the dream was no more.

We need a solid foundation if we are to follow the highest and best we know. Because when the storms of doubt and despair blast our structure, we will crumble if there isn't something solid underneath.

As I write this I'm tempted to quit, to turn back from the direction I chose some years back. All the advantages of giving up are looming seductively before me like water before a man dying of thirst. How strong is the desire to quit!

But I will not quit. I can't. Because I know nothing worthwhile can be accomplished by quitting. I may never accomplish all I would like to, but I will accomplish nothing if I give up.

And when I made my decision, I wasn't promised peaches and cream. The One I follow was crucified. Why should I think following Him will be easy? No, I made my vow to be faithful. And that is all He desires of me. Not to be successful. Not to be popular. But to be faithful.

I can do that. I can be faithful. I can hang in there and give the best I have. I will be a better person by doing that. And stronger. And by doing so I may help another who is struggling to stay above water.

Quit? Sure I want to quit. But I will not do that, no

matter how great the temptation. He is depending on me to be faithful. And that one thing I can and will do. I will not disappoint Him. I will be faithful.

Give me a drink of the Living Water. I'm ready to get back into the game of life!

THE DARK PERIODS OF LIFE

"Lo, I am with you always."
(Matthew 28:20)

I once read of a little girl's experience in riding a train through tunnels. The first time she was on a train that passed through a tunnel she scooted really close to her mother and held on for dear life. But after a few train-riding experiences the little girl was much more relaxed. One day, after exiting a tunnel, she turned to her mother and remarked, "Mother, I like tunnels!" Surprised, the mother asked why. The child replied, "Because tunnels have light at both ends!"

We must pass through many tunnels in life—tunnels of pain, disappointment, sorrow, and grief. In the midst of life's tunnels, when it is the blackest, there are some things we need to remember.

One is that God is with us, working for us, even when we aren't aware of His presence. God doesn't hang out a sign that says "The Almighty at work." He goes about His business unseen, unheard, and often unnoticed. He's like the majority of people responsible for the production of a movie. They work behind the scenes, putting the pieces together so the movie will have meaning.

We should also remember that God is with us even when we don't "feel" His presence. Often the presence of God is more of a conviction than it is a feeling. Sometimes the pain is so great in the tunnel that we're unaware of God's presence. But tunnels have light at both ends. Keep traveling. Don't stop.

Another thing we need to remember when in a tunnel is this: Even when we fail to ask, God continues to help. Sometimes the hurt in life is so deep that we can't utter well-worded prayers as we normally would. Perhaps we even fail to think of God. Does a parent always wait to be asked by a child before beginning to help? Of course not. Neither does God.

If we have given our life to God and have tried our best to be faithful to Him, it isn't His nature to run out on us simply because we temporarily forget to ask for His help. Life is a dark tunnel when we're dealt a hard blow. But God continues to help, even if we fail to ask Him to. There is light at both ends. Keep moving.

One final thought about God will help us in life's tunnels: Even when we doubt, He is still steadily working to help us. His ability to heal our hurt isn't totally dependent on our capacity to believe He can. God isn't limited by our finite minds, or even by our doubtful hearts. God is often helping us even when we say He can't help us.

Arthur John Gossip was a well-known Scottish preacher from Aberdeen. After his wife's unfortunate death he preached a sermon entitled "When Life Tumbles In, What Then?" In it he said, "I cannot comprehend how in trouble and loss and bereavement people can peevishly fling away their Christian faith. . . . Have we not lost enough without losing that too? . . . You people in the sunshine *may* believe the faith, but we in the shadow *must* believe it."

When passing through a tunnel, remember that there is light at both ends.

PART XI

THE CARPENTER LEADS ME ON

FOLLOW THE LEADER

"And if the blind leads the blind, both will fall into a ditch." (Matthew 15:14)

In Kuala Lumpur, a cross-country race was held. The race was to cover a seven-mile course. Two hours after the race had begun, ample time for the runners to cover the course, none of them had returned. The officials, fearing that something might have happened, set out in cars to find them.

They found all the runners six miles away, sprinting in the wrong direction. Many of them had already covered ten miles or more. The association secretary responsible for the race said the mix-up apparently occurred when the lead runner took a wrong turn at the fifth checkpoint and the rest followed.

Sometimes this happens to us. We follow the leader without knowing where the leader is going. We do things simply because someone else does them. We make our decision because someone else has made the same decision. And while this isn't always bad, it most certainly isn't always good.

All of us should be aware of where it is we're going. One of the worst mistakes so many in our society make is that they're running as fast as they can, following the person in front of them, trying desperately to catch up—and not knowing where the person they're following is headed.

Occasionally people come along who have considered where it is that they want to go. They stop long enough to study where following the person in front will lead. These people make up their own minds about which way the race should be going.

The Galilean Carpenter was like that. A full-fledged race was in progress when He came upon the scene. All the runners were following the leaders. They were pushing with all they had to keep up, to stay abreast with the crowd. The leaders had chosen their path, and the followers never questioned its correctness. They simply took for granted that the runner in front was going the right way.

Then He came into the race. He saw where those who were supposed to be leading the race were headed, and He knew that theirs was not the path that the Father had set for the race. So He stopped, noted the roads, and headed off in another direction. Because He was the leader in this new direction, the leaders that were going the other way became angry with Him. Why didn't He follow them like all the other runners? Of course, the only thing to do was to belittle Him and eventually get rid of Him. He could prove dangerous to the course they were leading.

This same idea of following the leader that prevailed back then is still around today. If the first car passes an injured person on the highway, all the other drivers generally do the same. If one person makes a joke about Christian values, all the others do too. If one shuns a person of another color, then everyone else shuns him. It's a game we play. We call it Follow the Leader.

I think I'd rather chart my own course than blindly follow the person in front of me.

DEALING WITH PROBLEMS

"I know what it is to be in need and what it is to have more than enough. I have learned this secret, so that anywhere, at any time, I am content, whether I am full or hungry, whether I have too much or too little. I have the strength to face all conditions by the power that Christ gives me." (Philippians 4:12–13 TEV)

We need to take life one day at a time. By this I don't mean that we shouldn't plan ahead, but that today is the only one we are to live *now*.

And, in a like manner, we should take only one problem at a time.

There is a story of a plumber in a town of about three thousand families. Winter brought a hard freeze, and all the pipes in the town burst. The plumber considered the situation and, realizing that he was the town's only plumber, decided that the job was too big for him to handle.

Night and day he worried how he would repair all the burst pipes in the town. Finally he threw up his hands in despair and told his wife he was going for a walk to forget his problems.

While he was out walking, a friend spotted him and asked him to please come into the house and repair his pipes. Because the man was a friend, the plumber couldn't refuse. When he was nearly through with the job, his friend's neighbor came over and asked the plumber to fix *his* pipes.

The plumber soon sent word home for his wife to have a good supper on the table, for he was working hard. After he fixed those pipes, there was another plea for assistance. Soon the plumber forgot the immensity of the problem and began solving it—one house at a time.

Looking at all our problems at one time, they seem impossible to overcome, and we're ready to give up in despair. But when we take them one at a time, we can usually cope.

The Carpenter said, "So don't worry about tomorrow; it will have enough worries of its own. There is no need to add to the troubles each day brings."

Live one day at a time, and face one problem at a time.

THE BEST ANSWER TO CRITICS

"But I say to you who hear: Love your enemies, do good to those who hate you." (Luke 6:27)

Edwin M. Stanton lived from 1814 to 1869. He was a nervous, asthmatic, cranky, and contradictory lawyer who worked his way up through the political ranks after dropping out of college because of a lack of funds. Stanton served as attorney general in the cabinet of President James Buchanan.

Stanton was also a sharp critic of Abraham Lincoln and had many unkind words for the man who followed Buchanan as the president of the United States. He called Lincoln "a low, cunning clown" and even nicknamed him "the original gorilla." Stanton went so far as to suggest to a famous hunter of the time that he was a fool to wander over Africa trying to catch a gorilla when he could easily bag one in Springfield, Illinois.

After being elected president, Lincoln was influential

in Stanton's acquiring a post as legal adviser to Simon Cameron, secretary of war. Even after this favor, Stanton continued his harsh criticism of Lincoln.

Many people were shocked when Lincoln appointed Stanton as the secretary of war following Cameron's resignation. It was hard for them to understand why Lincoln would give such an important post to a man who had continually criticized him and his policies.

While Stanton scoffed at Lincoln, Lincoln continued to show Stanton every courtesy. He never spoke to him harshly or returned hateful remarks with hateful remarks. Lincoln appointed Stanton secretary of war for one simple reason—Stanton was the best man for the job. Lincoln knew this and didn't let Stanton's criticisms stop him from making the appointment.

On the night of April 14, 1865, Lincoln was watching a play entitled *Our American Cousin* from a box at Ford's Theater in Washington. During the play, a man named John Wilkes Booth entered the box where Lincoln was sitting and shot the president in the head. Lincoln was carried to a nearby boardinghouse, where every attempt was made to save his life.

Into his room that night came several people. They watched—stunned—as their president lay dying. Among those present was Edwin Stanton, the man who had been so harshly critical of Lincoln, despite the fact that Lincoln had shown him every courtesy and kindness. Looking down at the rugged form of that gentle man, Stanton spoke through tears, saying, "There lies the greatest ruler of men the world has ever seen."

A Galilean Carpenter once said, "Love your enemies and pray for your persecutors and those who treat you spitefully." Stanton learned that this was the highest and noblest way of living ever given to the world. His criticism was finally silenced by love.

THE GREATEST PART OF THE FAITH

"And He said to them, 'Go into all the world and preach the gospel to every creature.'"
(Mark 16:15)

I made what was, to me, a startling discovery recently. I was reading about what happened on that Good Friday in Jerusalem nearly two thousand years ago. I read again how they hung that Man among men on those two sticks of wood. I could feel the blows of the hammer as they drove the nails into His palms. I could feel the jolt as the cross was dropped into its hole and came to rest. I could feel the flesh rip, see the blood spill. I could hear the crowd jeer, hear onlookers dare Him to come down from the cross.

But the story didn't end on that dark day. Finding an unused tomb in a garden nearby, His followers laid Him in it. And on Sunday those who loved Him found what all who have loved Him since have found: An empty tomb.

I said I made what was to me a startling discovery. All my life I had thought of the cross and that empty tomb as the most significant events in history. I had always considered these the top jewels on Jesus' crown of greatness. But now I see that they weren't the greatest part of His faith. Now I can see what the greatest part of this Carpenter's faith is. And it's amazing!

He entrusted the work of His Church to those eleven men, those disciples, who had just prior to the Resurrection betrayed Him! That, without a doubt, is the grandest thing about Him, that He trusted common people with the responsibility of His Gospel. Can you see that? Can you understand what it means? That He should give the greatest responsibility ever known to mankind to these eleven is without question the highest sign of his love and trust in us.

He entrusted His kingdom not to the high and mighty, to the great and gallant, to the brave and brilliant, but to common people! And He goes on entrusting his Church to plain, ordinary folk.

How great His trust in us! That He should give to common people the tremendous privilege of carrying on His work speaks to His great trust in us. No one would have dared to trust those eleven men with a great responsibility except that Nazarene. No one else has such a trust in common folk like you and me.

Next time you are inclined to lose hope in the human race, think about that.

THE HALFWAY PLACE

"Now when Paul and his party set sail from Paphos, they came to Perga in Pamphylia; and John, departing from them, returned to Jerusalem." (Acts 13:13)

Years ago, a story was told by the keeper of the Half Way House near Oberammergau in the Bavarian Alps. He said, "My Half Way House isn't a very happy place, and my job is not a very happy job." He told the reason.

A great number of people would enthusiastically start to climb the mountain. By the time they had reached his Half Way House, much of their enthusiasm had vanished and they found his place a welcome relief. The view from the Half Way House was beautiful, and the warmth and food dampened their desire to go back out into the cold and try to reach the top.

So many of those who reached the Half Way House

would settle there. They would not continue their journey to the top of the mountain. But these people were a restless group. They would be half-glad they had stayed inside the warm building and half-sad that they had not persevered to the top of the mountain. When the climbers who reached the top returned, those who had remained behind were miserable.

Do you remember the story of Terah? Remember how he took his family and set out from Ur of the Chaldeans to go to Canaan, the promised land? But when he got as far as Haran, five hundred miles from Ur and an equal distance from Canaan, Terah lost the vision and settled down. Scripture says simply, "Terah died in Haran."

It was Abraham, the son of Terah, who kept the vision alive and led his people to Canaan, the land of milk and honey. It is often the son who finishes the dream of the father, because many times the father becomes too comfortable at the halfway place.

Or take the case of Ned Boyle. Back in the late forties and early fifties, a foreign-car manufacturer was trying to get a foothold in the United States. The results weren't too encouraging. Then Ned Boyle assumed the advertising responsibility of that little car. And it wasn't long before Volkswagen "Bugs" were parked under the carports of thousands of homes around the country.

Officials for a rent-a-car firm that was way down the list approached Ned Boyle about taking their account. Competition was stiff. Many other companies were entering the rent-a-car market at the same time. But before long Avis Rent-a-Car proudly boasted: "We're Number Two. We try harder." When asked why he took a fledgling company that most people had counted out, Boyle answered, "I've always liked the challenge of making winners out of losers."

As Boyle discovered, the thrill is in accepting the challenge, climbing to the top of the mountain. Never stop halfway!

YOU DON'T HAVE TO COME BACK

"There is no fear in love; but perfect love casts out fear." (1 John 4:18)

Off the New England coast, there are several places where ships would be in danger if they should be caught in a storm. A story has arisen from that area about a crew of men whose responsibility was to rescue the men on any ship that ran into trouble there.

A storm came up out at sea, and the wind was blowing hard. The waves were extremely high and forceful. The storm was accompanied by heavy rain and much lightning. It was the middle of the night when the call came in to the rescue squad that a ship was in trouble and needed help evacuating her crew.

The captain of the rescue squad woke his men and told them to prepare to sail. As the group went out into the night, many of the men realized that it would be very dangerous to attempt to rescue in such conditions. Still the men were prepared to cast off and help the ship in distress.

Just before they cleared the safety of the harbor, a new member of the crew approached the captain. His face expressed much concern as he spoke.

"Sir," he said to the captain, "do you think we should go out in these conditions? We might not come back."

The old captain, a veteran of many years at aiding ships in distress, turned to the young seaman and gave his reply. "We don't have to come back, son. But we do have to go out."

Too often in life, the fear of failure keeps us from setting sail on a course of goodness. We're afraid we might not be successful in our venture. So we stay in the safety of the harbor.

Few great and worthwhile missions can be accomplished without taking the risk of sailing through some stormy seas. There is always the chance that we might not return. And it is that risk that keeps many people from leaving the shore.

When Columbus set sail for India he had no assurance that he would return. Indeed, he was told by many people that he would sail off the edge of the world and his ships would never stop falling. But he had to go, because he was captured by a dream, a dream that could change the life of people for the good.

When Jesus began his journey from Galilee to Jerusalem, His disciples probably tried to discourage him. They knew of the possibility that He would be killed in that holy city, that He would never come back. But still He went. He didn't have to come back. He only had to go.

Quite often in life we find this to be true. We don't have to come back. We only have to go.